Display
Electronics

No. 861
$8.95

Display Electronics
By Ken Tracton

TAB BOOKS
Blue Ridge Summit, Pa. 17214

Preface

Display devices are the mainstay of science, for without displays, scientists could not easily make observations and interpret data. I have always been fascinated by the variety of forms that displays can have and how they can represent data. In fact, this very fascination has led me to experiment with display systems capable of providing a clearer and more precise picture of reality.

I was greatly inspired by the advent of the light-emitting diode and its cousin, the solid-state photodetector. Amazingly, the LED is the mystical "cold light" spoken of in older science fiction stories. So this book grew directly out of an appreciation for the cold-light devices and the many other comtemporary displays.

I would like to sincerely thank the following companies that supplied data, materials, and constructive advice: General Electric, Hamlin, Hewlett-Packard, Monsanto, Opcoa, and Xciton. I must thank John Striloff who drew all the original diagrams for my notes, and a special thank-you goes to Jack and Lorraine who showed me the light.

Ken Tracton

Contents

Chapter 1

Photon Emission, Transmission, and Detection

Solid-state light-emitting devices, whether they are discrete units or comprise entire arrays, have some very desirable features that include reliability, stability, ruggedness, low power consumption, and longevity. Another interesting feature is that solid-state devices are almost monochromatic (single color), which is attributed to the fact that their emitted radiation is distributed over a very narrow bandwidth. The color, of course, may be changed by the fabrication process to yield a variety of colors for different applications. And because of their inherent solid structure, such exemplary devices as light-emitting diodes (LEDs) can be built with integral lenses to magnify and focus the light.

The ability of a material to produce a "cold" light has been known for almost 70 years, but only recently have practical devices entered the electronics realm. The earliest reported incidence of solid-state light emission was with a crystal of carborundum (silicon carbide, SiC). As compared with modern light-emitting diodes, the carborundum crystal required a potential of almost 30V where today's LEDs require only a few volts.

The introduction of the LED has greatly enhanced electronics, particularly in the areas of indicators, readouts, and in remote control devices. One of the many varieties of LEDs is the semiconductor injection laser. Unfortunately, most injection laser diodes operate in the pulse mode only, yet a few diodes have been designed recently that will operate continuously at ordinary room temperatures.

The solid-state readout has caused the older multiplace (one character in front of the other) glow tube readout to be almost extinct now. Where the glow tube was ambiguous in its ability to represent a number or figure without confusion, the LED readout matrix presents any of its readout characters in the same plane. The glow tubes and filament readouts that operated in one plane consume much more power both in terms of increased voltage requirements and current drain. The liquid crystal readout may seem to be in direct opposition to the LED readout, but the liquid crystal readout does not generate light; therefore, a light source is required with these readouts.

PHOTON MEASUREMENT

To incorporate an effective discussion on light-emitting or light-sensitive devices, it is best to define and understand the different concepts involved.

Many individuals will call any radiant energy "light." This is technically incorrect as light is only that part of the electromagnetic spectrum that is perceivable by the human eye. The electromagnetic spectrum in its entirety and the section that is considered to be light is shown in Fig. 1-1. Light is often defined as *visually* evaluated radiant energy.

To be able to discuss both perceivable and nonperceivable radiant energy, two different systems of measurements have evolved. These two systems are *photometric* and *radiometric*. Photometric is a method of *visible* energy parameter evaluation. Radiometric is the system used for measuring energy *anywhere* in the electromagnetic spectrum.

In the radiometric system, the strength of a given emission is described in terms of its power, or total *flux density*; its period (or wavelength) rather than frequency is used. But in photometry, the effect upon the eye is the deciding factor in determining the strength of a wave.

The units used for photometric measurements are weighted according to the physiological effect the flux or flux density has. Quite often the wavelength is described in terms of its color, such as red, blue, and green. Such colors as ultraviolet, black light, or infrared light are used without

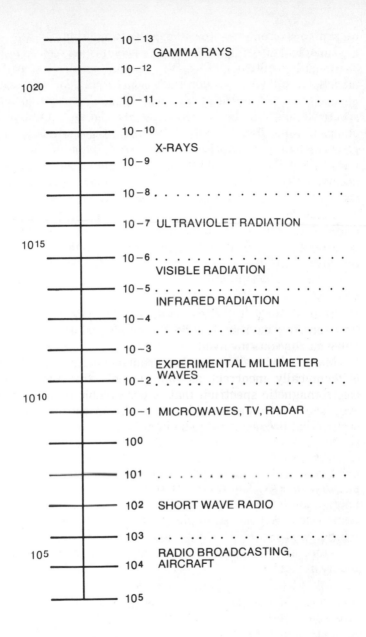

FREQUENCY .... WAVELENGTH
(HERTZ)   (METERS)

Fig. 1-1. The electromagnetic wave spectrum.

regard to photometry, for if a given wavelength causes no physiological effect upon the human eye, it is not termed light. Technically, ultraviolet (UV) should never be called ultraviolet *light* but rather ultraviolet *radiation*. The same applies to the infrared portion of the electromagnetic spectrum; it should be termed infrared *radiation*. As far as the popular name "black light" (UV) goes, the name itself is a give-away that the expression is in error; for if the "light" is truly "black," how would you see it? The terms just mentioned are normally used to indicate those wavelengths that are near the *perceivable* portion of the electromagnetic spectrum.

In order for us to discuss a light device accurately, we must use radiometric units. These units must be adjusted according to the response curve of the measurement device we are using. In light detectors an important parameter is *effective irradiance*, which is measured in terms of the *flux density* (e.g., watts per square centimeter) falling on the receiving surface. For broadband radiation having a spectral distribution of energy E_λ, the total *effective* energy may be found by breaking up the band into many narrow bands, then multiplying the energy in each narrow band by the relative *detector response* $D(\lambda)$ in that band. Then we merely add the resulting *effective* energies together.

$$E_{\text{EFF}} = \Sigma D(\lambda) E_\lambda \, \Delta\lambda \quad \text{watts/cm}^2$$

Energy from a given source that lies outside the response band of the detector we are using does not contribute to the effective energy. Therefore, the relationship between effective energy and total energy is dependent on the source of energy being used. A good example is radiation at or around 1.0 micron in wavelength; it is 100% effective upon a silicon detector but 0% effective upon the human eye, making it totally invisible.

Table 1-1 shows the relationships between the radiometric and the photometric systems of measurements. To differentiate between symbols that are the same for both systems, the subscript *V* will be used for the photometric (visual) and a subscript *E* for the radiometric (physical). Also shown are the commonly used units for each parameter.

Both infrared radiation (IR) and visible light sources are involved in the use of silicon light detectors. The table gives

Table 1-1. Radiometric and Photometric Units

TERMINOLOGY	RADIOMETRIC	PHOTOMETRIC
Total flux	Φ_E(watts)	Φ_V(lumens)
Flux density emitted from a surface	M_E(watt/cm^2) radiant emittance	M_V(lumen/cm^2) luminous emittance
Incident flux density on a surface	E_E(watt/cm^2) irradiance	E_V(lumen/cm^2) illumination
Source intensity	I_E(watt/steradian) radiant intensity	I_V(watt/steradian) luminous intensity
Incident flux per unit solid angle falling on surface	L_E(watt/cm^2-steradian) radiance	L_V(lumen/cm^2-steradian) luminance

the radiometric and photometric terminology needed in a discussion of sources and detectors. Each photometric term may be derived from the corresponding radiometric term by integration of the product of spectral distribution and multiplying by the spectral response of the human eye. The total luminous flux Φ_V is related to the total radian flux Φ_E by the formula

$$\Phi_V = K_M \int \Phi_E(\lambda)V(\lambda)d\lambda \quad \text{lumens}$$

where K_M is a proportional constant that is equal to 680 lumens/watt for $\Phi_E(\lambda)$ in watts per unit wavelength. Φ_V is in lumens and $V(\lambda)$ is the relative sensitivity of the human eye to light of different wavelengths.

Similarly, illumination E_V is related to irradiance E_E by the equation

$$E_V = K_M \int E_E(\lambda)V(\lambda)d\lambda \quad \text{lumens/cm}^2$$

where $E_E(\lambda)$ is in watts/cm^2 per unit wavelength.

To produce a certain eye response, the effective incident radiation required is the illumination E_V. To produce a certain response in a detector, a similiar concept is used to derive the term E_{EFF}, which represents the effective incident radiation (flux density) necessary.

The development of the light-emitting diode and related light detectors has made investigation into optical communication shift into high gear. Generally speaking, an optical system consists of a modulated or pulsed light source

Table 1-2. Point Source Parameters

PARAMETER	RADIOMETRIC	PHOTOMETRIC
Source intensity	I_E (watts/steradian)	I_V (lumens/steradian)
Flux through receiving surface	$\Phi_E = I_E A/r^2$ (watts)	$\Phi_V = I_V A/r^2$ (lumens)
Incident flux intensity	$E_E = \Phi_E/A = I_E/r^2$ (watts/square unit)	$E_V = I_V/r^2$ (lumens/square unit)
Total flux output	$\Phi_{ET} = 4\pi I_E$ (watts)	$\Phi_{VT} = 4\pi I_V$ (lumens)
Receiver surface inclined at angle θ	$E_E = I_E/r^2 \cos(\theta)$ (watts/square unit)	$E_V = I_V/r^2 \cos(\theta)$ (lumens/square unit)

and a detector of this source. The optical source can be an incandescent lamp or a semiconductor light-emitting diode, while the detector can be a photodiode, a phototransistor, or another light-dependent device.

Table 1-2 lists some of the relationships of sources of visible and invisible energy. Figures 1-2 and 1-3 show what the various parameters mean. When energy is emitted from a point source, it travels outward in all directions. For purposes of measurement, the irradiated surface is normally a

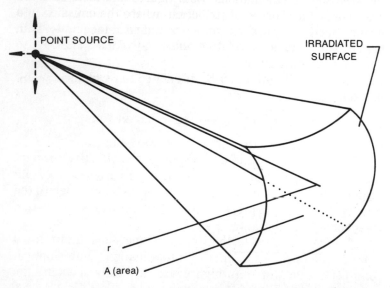

Fig. 1-2. A surface irradiated by the theoretical point source.

spherical one, and the surface area of a sphere equals $4\pi r^2$ where r is the radius of the sphere. A *steradian* is a "solid" angle related to the surface area of the sphere. By definition, the total surface area of a sphere is 4π steradians, and one steradian is equal to the surface area of the sphere divided by the square of the sphere's radius, or A/r^2. Figure 1-2 shows how a point source irradiates a portion of the spherical surface. Figure 1-3 illustrates the parameters involved when the irradiated surface of the receiver is tilted at an angle θ with respect to the incident radiation. As in Table 1-1, a subscript E indicates a radiometric symbol and a subscript V a photometric symbol.

Intensity (angular flux density) is the flux per unit solid angle emitted from the source along radial lines, unless lenses or reflectors are used to redirect the flux. Even in the extreme case of narrow beam concentration, the beam is divergent over a sufficiently long distance, so the concept of angular flux density still applies. Of course, if the beam were perfectly collimated, the term *intensity* would be useless, and we would use the term *flux per unit area*, which would remain constant regardless of distance.

After examining point sources, the obvious next step is to look at area sources. Table 1-3 and Figs. 1-4 and 1-5 give data for area-source calculations. Both figures and table data are based on a Lambertian distribution, where the emission in a given direction is proportional to the cosine of the angle θ with respect to the normal direction (the perfect diffuser).

The incident flux density is reduced by the cosine of angle θ with respect to the normal, if the direction under consideration is not normal to the emitting surface. Rather

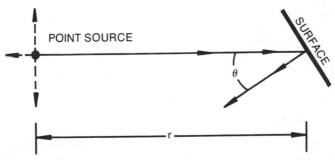

Fig. 1-3. An angle θ exists between incident and reflected radiation from a surface.

Table 1-3. Area Source Parameters (Perfect Diffuser)

PARAMETER	RADIOMETRIC	PHOTOMETRIC
Source intensity per area normal to surface	$L_E=$(watts/steradian-cm^2)	$L_V=$(lumens/steradian-cm^2)
Emitted flux density incident flux density	$M_E=\pi L_E$(watts/cm^2) $E_E=\dfrac{L_E\pi r^2}{r^2+d^2}$ $=\dfrac{L_E A_S}{r^2+d^2}$ (watts/cm^2)	$M_V=\pi L_V$(lumens/cm^2) $E_V=\dfrac{\pi L_V L_V A_S(\text{lumens/cm}^2)}{r^2+d^2}$
Total flux output	$\Phi=M_E A_S$(watts)	$\Phi_V=M_V A_S$ (lumens)

Note: If r is less than d/10, the area source can be consider a point source of intensity, where
$I_E=L_E A_S$ watts/steradian and $I_V=L_V A_S$ lumens/steradian

than the actual surface area, this condition is equivalent to using the projected area of the source in that direction. The projected area is easily found, whereas the actual area may be quite impossible to determine for irregular surface profiles.

We have already discussed to some degree the different parameters that we will measure when dealing with light sources and receptors, but to further this knowledge, a deeper insight into the physics of light itself is needed.

LIGHT

It is without a doubt that one of the most important concepts that came into being in the 19th century was the fact that light was an electromagnetic wave. Electromagnetic waves, consisting of magnetic fields and electric fields interacting, were theorized by James Clerk Maxwell around

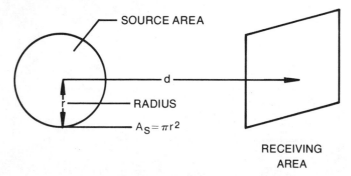

Fig. 1-4. A surface irradiated by an area source.

1864. Upon further investigation, Maxwell realized that since electromagnetic waves are transversal—as are light waves—and they both had the same velocity in a vacuum, then electromagnetic waves and light waves must be one and the same phenomenon. This theory has since been checked and verified in every possible way.

Electromagnetic induction occurs when a changing magnetic field produces an electric field. Similarly, an electric field that is varying will produce a magnetic field. A magnetic field does not correspond directly to an electric field, but the important point is that it is impossible to have a varying electric field without a magnetic field associated with it, and it is impossible to have a varying magnetic field without its accompanying electric field. Using this hypothesis, Maxwell was able to develop a theory of the operation of field fluctuations and their ability to transverse a vacuum (space).

The first theory to come forward from these hypotheses was that electromagnetic waves spread out from a disturbance rather like the way waves spread out across water when the surface is disturbed. When electromagnetic waves spread out from an electric or magnetic disturbance, their energy is constantly changing from electric fields to magnetic fields. Figure 1-6 shows an artist's concept of an electromagnetic field; keep in mind that in reality a real electromagnetic field is three-dimensional.

There are three important factors to remember when considering electromagnetic fields:

1—The variations or fluctuations are occurring simultaneously for both the electric and the magnetic

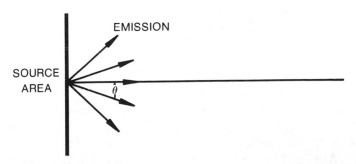

Fig. 1-5. Emission distributed in one hemisphere is related to cos (θ).

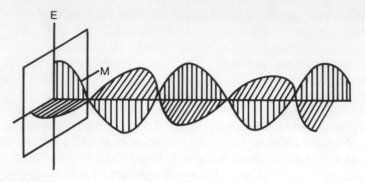

Fig. 1-6. Electromagnetic radiation consists of a magnetic and an electric field both perpendicular to each other and to the direction of propagation.

fields. Therefore the maxima and minima of the two fields appear at the same time and the same place.

2—The directions of the two fields are at right angles to each other; that is, the electric field is perpendicular to the magnetic. Both fields are also perpendicular to the direction they are moving in. Therefore, light waves are *transversal*.

3—The speed of the electromagnetic wave depends only upon the magnetic and electric properties of the medium the wave is transversing, not upon the amplitudes of the two fields.

Another thing to consider is that in electromagnetic waves nothing material moves, as opposed to sound waves where the medium moves or where waves move in water. In the case of electromagnetic waves, nothing moves in the path of the wave, the only thing that changes is the field intensities.

The velocity of an electromagnetic wave (light) is usually represented by the letter c, which has a value of 2.998×10^8 m/sec. This figure is usually accepted as 3×10^8 m/sec for most calculations.

Of all the many possible frequencies in the electromagnetic spectrum, light occupies only a very small section or band. This band spans the frequencies from 3×10^{12} Hz (red) to 8×10^{12} Hz (violet). Only frequencies between these two boundaries are visible to the human eye.

As stated earlier, *wavelength* is normally used to describe a given wave, rather than its *frequency*. The formula used to

18

obtain wavelength from frequency is:

$$\lambda = c/f$$

where λ is the wavelength, c is the speed of light, and f is the frequency.

Refraction

Light was understood to be a wave phenomenon long before the theory connecting it with electromagnetic radiation was set forward. Many people have set forth the theory that light was indeed a wave, while others have had the theory that light was a particle phenomenon. But before we get deeper into this discussion, let's review some simple experiments and observations.

If a light beam passes *obliquely* from one medium to the next, it is deflected to some degree at the surface between the two media. In optical physics this effect is regarded in terms of angles with respect to the normal to the medium. The *normal* is the angle perpendicular to the surface of the medium at the point where the beam enters the medium.

If a light beam enters the water at the same angle as the normal, no deflection occurs (Fig. 1-7). If light enters the water medium at any angle other than that of the normal, the light is bent *towards* the normal at the point of entry. Of course, this effect works in both directions. If light leaves the water at an angle other than that of the normal, it will bend away from the normal at the point of entry into the air medium. This property of light bending when entering one medium and leaving another medium is called *refraction*.

Now what does this have to do with whether light is composed of particles or waves? The best way to examine this situation is to try to fit the particle theory and then the wave theory to the refraction observation. According to the particle theory, the velocity of a light beam entering the water from an oblique angle may be considered as composed of two vectors, one vector parallel to the normal and the other vector parallel to the surface of the water.

If we assume that light is composed of particles, we can further assume that some force will be exerted on the light particles as they enter the water. The direction of this force should be normal to the surface so that it will have no bending effect on light particles traveling normal to the surface, but

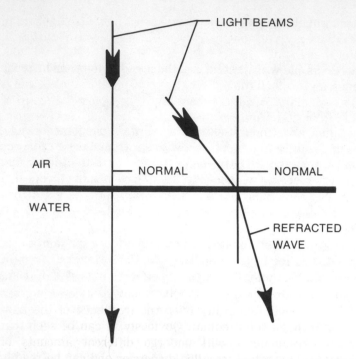

Fig. 1-7. As electromagnetic radiation crosses the interface between two media, refraction occurs to change its direction of propagation.

will have maximum effect as particles approach parallel to the surface. The force vector would logically act to slow the light as it enters the water and speed the light as it enters the air going in the other direction. The resultant observation is that the light beam always bends with respect to the normal. Moreover, the velocity of light would be slower in water than in air.

Now let's examine the wave theory. If two or more rays of light enter the water at an oblique angle, obviously the ray closest to the water enters first. Of course, we assume that the rays of light travel parallel to each other while in air or while in water. If light waves travel slower in water than in air, the ray that entered the water first will travel a shorter distance in the water than the other rays are traveling in the air until they reach the water's surface. The rays will then continue traveling parallel to each other again. Obviously, the angle now between the normal and the rays will be smaller than when in the air. Since this is indeed the effect that is observed when light enters water, we can say that light also appears to behave as a wave and that this wave would travel slower in water than in air.

The problem of whether light is actually slower or faster in a medium in which the light is refracted towards the normal is easy to explain. But the experiment to measure the speed of light in water and air is rather difficult to perform. Nevertheless, after due experimentation it was finally proven that light did indeed slow upon entering the water, thereby giving greater credit to the wave theory.

The index of refraction (n) of a given medium is calculated from the ratio between the speed of light in a vacuum (c) and its speed (v) in that given medium, or

$$n = c/v$$

The greater the value of n, the greater the extent to which a light beam will be deflected. The highest frequencies have the greatest value of n because the index of refraction for a given medium depends generally upon the frequency of the light passing through the medium. Obviously, it can be seen that different frequencies will undergo different amounts of deflection. This effect is called *dispersion* and can be readily observed in a prism. The band of colors that leaves the prism is called the visible spectrum.

Diffraction

The next important attribute of light is diffraction. Diffraction is the ability of a wave to bend around the edge of an obstacle in its path. Certainly, a beam of particles cannot behave as waves in the manner required to produce this phenomenon. And because a sharp outline is usually observed in a shadow, it was at one time believed that this was proof enough that light was composed of particles because no observable diffraction was occurring.

Diffraction, however, is only readily visible when the obstacle or aperture in the obstacle is comparable in dimensions to a wavelength of the light being used. Measuring diffraction of light is thus difficult, but not so with sound. The velocity of sound through water, for example, is considerably slower than light, and wavelengths of one meter or so are easily obtained. Wavelengths of sound in air are somewhat smaller. It is not hard to see why diffraction was not observed earlier with light when the typical wavelength is about 10^{-6} meter.

Interference

Stronger support for the wave theory of light was found in the fact that light beams could behave in a manner called *interference*. Interference is easy to understand. If two light beams travel past the same point at the same time, the total amplitude of the light beam is the sum of the two beams. Therefore, if the beams are *in phase* with each other, they will have a greater total amplitude, and if they are *out of phase*, they will have a smaller total amplitude.

To be *in phase* simply means that the crest of one wave meets the crest of the other wave. In Fig. 1-8 we see constructive interference in part A and destructive interference in B. Figure 1-8C shows the parts of the wave called the *crest* and *trough*. If two waves meet that are of different frequencies, they periodically combine to form constructive and destructive interference.

Transverse and Longitudinal Waves

A longitudinal wave is one in which the motion of the particles *parallel* to the direction of the wave is disturbed. Transverse waves affect the particles *perpendicular* to the

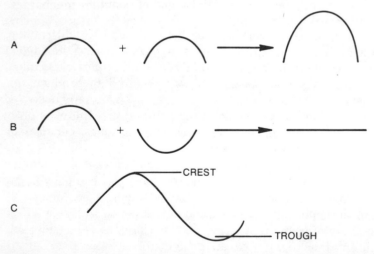

Fig. 1-8. Constructive interference (A) increases the wave amplitude, while destructive interference (B) decreases amplitude and may cause complete cancellation. (C) identifies the crest and trough portions of the wave.

wave direction. A good example of a longitudinal wave is that of sound. An example of a transverse wave is the wave that moves down a string of an instrument when plucked. Both longitudinal and transverse waves can experience refraction, diffraction, and interference.

Which type does light belong to? The ability to be *polarized* will give us the clue needed. When a wave's vibrations occur in only a single direction perpendicular to the direction in which the beam travels, this is a polarized transverse wave. In this condition the entire wave motion is confined to a plane called the *plane of polarization*. If many different directions of polarization occur in a given beam, that beam is deemed unpolarized. Obviously, since longitudinal waves vibrate in only one direction (that in which the wave is traveling), a longitudinal wave cannot be polarized. By definite experimentation it is easy to prove that light definitely can be polarized. So light is a transverse wave. If you will recall the diagram in Fig. 1-6 of the electromagnetic wave, you will note that both the electric and magnetic fields move perpendicularly to the direction of travel, and light is an electromagnetic wave.

PHOTOELECTRIC EFFECT

Let's consider light from still another aspect, brought about by the theory of relativity and of quantum mechanics. Both relativity and quantum theory altered the view of physics to a great degree.

Just before these two theories were put forward, experimentation produced an interesting effect—that electrons are emitted from the surface of a metal when exposed to light. This emission of electrons was found to be more noticeable if the light used was in the ultraviolet portion of the electromagnetic spectrum. This phenomenon became known as the *photoelectric effect*, and the electrons being emitted are called *photoelectrons*.

If you observe this phenomenon rather casually, the electron emission is not out of the ordinary. Light waves do carry energy. If this energy is somehow absorbed by the metal surface electrons, you would expect that certain electrons would escape as the photoenergy is transformed into kinetic energy. Unfortunately, on detailed examination, this simple explanation does not quite hold water.

The intensity of the light falling on the metal surface has very little effect on the *energy* of the emitted electrons. Obviously, a more intense light source will yield more electrons than a less intense source, but the average energy of the electrons remains the same. Even if a very dim light source is introduced, electrons will still leave the metal surface immediately. This phenomenon clearly goes against the electromagnetic theory of light, which states effectively that the energy of the photoelectrons should depend upon the intensity of the light. If the light intensity is low enough, a considerable time should be required before a given electron has accumulated sufficient energy to escape the metallic surface.

Another problem is that the frequency of the light source seemed to play an important part in determining the energy content of the photoelectrons. From experimentation it was found that a critical *minimum* frequency was required to liberate photoelectrons from the surface, and this critical frequency depended upon the particular metal being illuminated. Once above this critical frequency, the energy of the photoelectrons being emitted increased with an increase of frequency. For example, a dim violet light would produce fewer but more energetic electrons than a very bright red light would. In equation form the maximum photoelectron energy (kinetic energy) is related to frequency by

$$E_{\text{MAX}} = h(f - f_0) = hf - hf_0$$

where E_{MAX} is maximum photoelectron energy, f_0 is the threshold frequency (critical minimum frequency) and depends upon the particular metal, and h which is a constant that will be discussed shortly.

Albert Einstein realized that the electromagnetic light theory fell short of explaining the photoelectric effect. In 1905, Einstein extrapolated a theory based on research done by Max Planck. Planck had done theoretical research on the radiation given off by a material that was heated to a point of incandescence. Planck found that physical laws would hold true for the emitted radiation as long as "the radiation was considered as being emitted in small bursts, rather than being emitted continuously."

Planck's little bursts came to be known as *quanta*. Planck was able to show that the energy of each *quantum* was related to the frequency of the light source by

$$E = hf$$

where E is the energy, f is the frequency, and h is a constant whose value is equal to 6.63×10^{-34} J-sec (h is now called Planck's constant).

It was Einstein who realized that light was not only emitted in quanta, but traveled *as* quanta. With this insight, Einstein postulated that the first equation discussed could be rewritten as;

$$hf = E_{MAX} + hf_0$$

There exists a critical minimum frequency f_0 (threshold frequency) that relates to the minimum energy required to release an electron from a surface of a given metal. All the electrons do not have the same energy (maximum energy) because not all the quantum energy hf may be transferred to a single electron. Of course, an electron can also lose energy by collisions within the metal before it reaches the surface and escapes.

These small units or packets of energy, which are referred to as quanta, are also called *photons*. Now if we have small units of energy traveling, it looks like light is a particle phenomenon by nature. But experimentation and reason point to waves. For example, diffraction and interference cannot be explained by any other way than wave theory! Quantum theory explains light as a succession of quanta (photons) spreading out from a source, where wave theory explains light energy being distributed evenly throughout the wave pattern.

A Contradiction?

It seems that the two theories about light contradict each other. If you consider the quantum theory closely, it does picture light as particles. If frequency is used to determine the quantum energy, which of course it does, the quantum theory also describes light in terms of waves since frequency is a wave phenomenon. Quantum theory also gives the correct explanation of the photoelectric effect, but wave theory cannot do so.

What theory should we believe in? Physics has had theories that required updating or replacement with new ideas, but this is the only ocurrence of a phenomenon that requires *two* theories that are completely different from each other. We must assume therefore that light behaves in certain ways as particles and in other ways as waves. Light can behave either way—but in no known physical process has light ever been observed as exhibiting both its natures at the same time. Therefore we can say that the electromagnetic and quantum theories complement each other in the explanation of what light is and how it behaves.

It must simply be remembered that light is a phenomenon that can manifest itself either as waves or as particles. We cannot "see" the true nature of light. If there is one, it may be explained by a new and single theory. Perhaps we will always have no choice but to accept two theories to account for the behavior of a single phenomenon.

So, with a better understanding of what a photon is, let's discuss photon emission.

Photon Emission

Photons are generated or produced by one of two different behavior modes. These behavior modes are very general in nature and will be discussed as such. The two basic mechanisms for light production are *luminescence* and *incandescence*.

Incandescence results from thermal energy (heat). For example, if electricity is passed through a resistive conductor, it will heat up and glow, giving off light energy. The thermal energy that is generated is measured in terms of temperature, usually in degrees Kelvin. This is an absolute temperature scale where 0°K is the absolute zero. The higher the temperature of the material, the greater the total radiation that will be emitted from the material and, of course, the greater the proportion that will be visible radiation (light). Other methods of heating a material may also be used to generate incandescence. But incandescence is the broadband visible radiation that is a function of the absolute temperature of the light source and increases in intensity as the temperature increases.

Luminescence is the general category of all light-producing mechanisms other than heat. Physicists generally label the type of luminescence by the method of excitation used. For example, electric current produces electroluminescence; chemicals, chemiluminescence; light, photoluminescence. Luminescence is usually a narrowband radiation emitted by a material or substance due to a change in energy levels (by electrons) caused by external excitation.

JUNCTION CHARACTERISTICS

In this book we are particularly interested in a special form of luminescence called *PN junction luminescence,* or *junction electroluminescence.* PN junction luminescence can be caused by application of direct current at a low voltage level to a properly doped semiconductor crystal having a PN junction. Basically, this process is a two-fold behavior: (1) excitation, where electrical energy is absorbed; (2) recombination, where the absorbed energy is released as heat and light.

The light-emitting diode (LED), sometimes called a solid-state lamp (SSL), is a specially prepared PN junction diode that emits light when biased in the forward direction. The radiation produced by the LED may range from the near ultraviolet, through the visible, and down to the far infrared region of the electromagnetic spectrum. As said before, the PN junction is specially prepared to emit electromagnetic radiation. To understand and visualize this special PN junction, let's consider some basic semiconductor behavior first.

Semiconductors

Most materials can be categorized generally as insulators, semiconductors, and conductors. These categories are based upon a substance's ability to conduct electricity. Materials like glass, ceramics, and the element sulphur are insulators; that is, they conduct an electric current rather poorly. Other materials such as the metals gold, silver, and copper are conductors and present very little resistance to a current flow. In between these two classes are the semiconductors, such as germanium and silicon, which are not as high in resistivity as the insulators, yet they are not as good conductors as the metals.

The ability of a material to conduct an electric current is dependent on the number of free electrons the material possesses. If the proportion of free electrons is high in the material, it is a conductor; if low, it is an insulator. Good conductors like copper (Fig. 1-9) are characterized by having

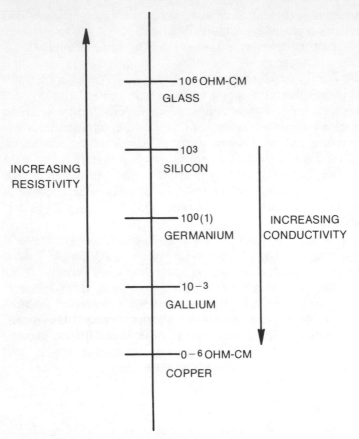

INCREASING
RESISTIVITY

10^6 OHM-CM
GLASS

10^3
SILICON

$10^0(1)$
GERMANIUM

10^{-3}
GALLIUM

0^{-6} OHM-CM
COPPER

INCREASING
CONDUCTIVITY

Fig. 1-9. Comparison of resistivities. (Resistivity is the reciprocal of conductivity.) Good conductors have high conductivity, while good insulators have high resistivity.

low resistivity and high conductivity. Good insulators like glass exhibit low conductivity and high resistivity.

In most semiconductor devices the material used in the fabrication of the devices must be tailored electrically. To do this, a crystalline piece of the semiconductor material is doped with atoms of some other element. Generally, the pure crystalline structure has poor current-carrying abilities. Thus, to obtain free electrons, an impurity is added with an atomic structure different than that of the "host" atom. This impurity will modify the crystal lattice such that current carriers are developed. Usually, the amount of impurities added are in very small proportion to that of the host, but even this small amount is sufficient to unbalance the number of "holes" and electrons in the original material.

A hole is defined as being the opposite of an electron—a space left where an electron was. Therefore, we can consider a hole to be of an electric positive charge equal but opposite to that of the electron.

There are two main classes of impurities (dopants). There are *acceptor* atoms, usually just called acceptors, which will *remove* electrons, thus creating holes. A semiconductor material made with acceptor atoms added is called P-type material. N-type material is made by adding *donor* atoms, called donors, which *add* electrons to the semiconductor.

PN Junctions

In the region where a P-type and a N-type semiconductor join, a PN junction is formed (see Fig. 1-10). As the N-type material contains free electrons and the P-type contains holes a charge diffusion will occur between the two sides. Some of the free electrons will diffuse across the PN junction and fill holes in the P-type material; this occurrence takes place adjacent to the PN junction only. After this diffusion occurs,

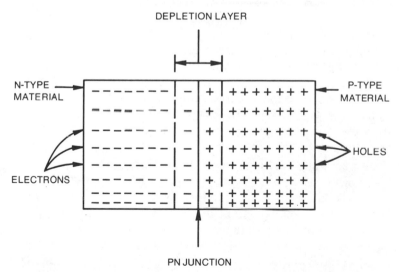

Fig. 1-10. The interface between the N and P materials is called a PN junction. Although the PN device may be thought of as a "sandwich" made of N and P materials, in reality the device is one solid piece of crystalline material in which only the amounts of doping materials vary in the region to either side of the junction region.

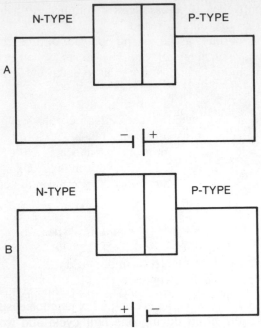

Fig. 1-11. Current will flow when the PN junction is forward biased (A) and will not flow when reverse biased (B).

which takes an incredibly short period of time, a space-charge region forms through the displacement of electrons.

The space-charge region can be thought of as a built-in electric field. Because of the electron displacement, the N-type material adjacent to the PN junction acquires a small positive charge, while the adjacent P-type semiconductor acquires a slight negative charge. This space charge (potential gradient) prevents any further diffusion.

A current flow can be made to pass through a PN junction if certain conditions are met first. If a direct current source such as a battery is applied to the PN junction, a current flow can be established. If the negative terminal of the battery is applied to the N-type side and the positive terminal of the battery is attached to the P-type material, electrons from the negative terminal will enter the N side and flow towards the PN junction. Electrons in the P-type material will flow towards the battery, leaving behind holes. Therefore we have the space-charge potential barrier decreasing, which will allow free electrons from the N-type material to enter the space-charge region, cross over the junction, and flow through the P-type semiconductor toward the positive terminal of the battery. This is called *forward biasing*—an electric current will flow.

If the poles of the battery are reversed so that the negative terminal is attached to the P-type material and the positive terminal is applied to the N-type semiconductor, a situation called *reverse biasing* occurs. Here, the free electrons of the N-type material are forced away from the PN junction and toward the positive battery terminal, while electrons from the negative terminal fill up the holes available in the P-type semiconductor. Obviously, the space-charge barrier will increase until it has a charge equal to that of the applied battery voltage. Since there is no voltage difference between the sides, no current will flow.

Figure 1-11 illustrates the two methods of biasing the PN junction. We can see therefore that a PN junction conducts easily in one direction and not in the other; thus we have the diode (rectifier). If, for example, an alternating current (AC) were applied, current would cross the PN junction easily in the forward-bias direction during one half cycle and would not flow during the other half cycle. Figure 1-12 shows the typical

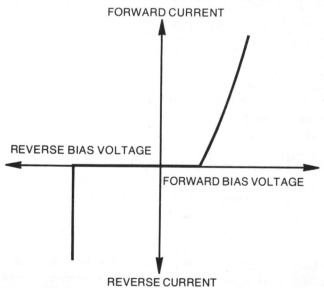

Fig. 1-12. Current increases as the applied voltage increases in the forward-bias mode. In the reverse-bias condition, once the critical voltage is reached, breakdown occurs and heavy current flow is observed.

curve associated with the PN junction, voltage-current characteristics. There are two points to remember: (1) excessive voltage in the reverse-bias condition can cause voltage breakdown; (2) excessive current in the forward-bias direction can cause overheating. In either case, these conditions can damage the semiconductor device to a point were it is no longer usable.

Energy Levels

Physics dictates that electrons in association with an atom are permitted only certain discrete and ordered energy levels. Energy values that are not permitted are forbidden, but this is true only for a free atom. If an accumulation of atoms occurs, such as in the case of a semiconductor material, the electrons associated with the atoms of the material tend to interact with the electrons of adjacent atoms. The energy levels are now considered to be "energy bands" because of this interaction. As with energy levels, energy bands are only allowed certain values, values in between are forbidden.

Any physical system tends to seek an equilibrium at its lowest energy level. Electrons fill these energy bands from lowest to highest, in that order. In a pure semiconductor there are two specific energy bands that we are interested in. These two energy bands are the *conduction* band and the *valence* band. Between these two energy bands exists the forbidden gap where no electrons are permitted. The highest band that is available to electrons to fill is the valence band. At temperatures approaching absolute zero ($0°K$), the valence band is filled with electrons from the conduction band above it. The conduction band is thus without any charge carriers that are free to conduct electric current.

If electrons completely fill the highest valence energy band and an electron jumps from one position to another, an electron from the position just occupied would jump back to fill the original position. We can easily see therefore that there would be no net current as there is no net flow of charge, and hence no conduction.

Obviously, the only way that current can flow in a material is if the conduction band is partially filled with electrons. With a partially filled conduction band, the electrons there are able to move freely in the band.

Doping a pure semiconductor with donor atoms produces an N-type material. At thermal equilibrium the lowest states of the conduction band contain free electrons. Doping a pure semiconductor with acceptor atoms produces a P-type crystalline material in which electrons from the valence band's highest states transfer over to the acceptor atoms, leaving holes.

Now let us apply this information towards photon (light) generation in a solid-state device.

Light Emission

Earlier we mentioned that light produced in a semiconductor by junction electroluminescence was a two-fold process. This process is called *injection recombination*. We will first consider the initial phase, or injection.

To get the electrons to flow in a semiconductor lamp from the N-type material to the P-type material (within the conduction band), the distribution equilibrium must be unbalanced. If an external DC power supply is applied with the proper polarities, as described earlier, the potential step or junction barrier potential will be reduced, causing electron (and hole) flow. (Holes flow in the valence band and electrons flow in the conduction band in semiconductor materials.)

With this electron-hole flow we get a condition known as *minority carrier injection*. This type of excitation will always expend energy. Electrons are pumped (injected) into the P-type material, which is filled with holes as the majority charge carriers. The holes are injected into the N-type material, which has electrons as the majority carriers. So we can see where the term *minority carrier injection* comes from. Obviously, the carriers are in minority in the material they are being pumped into.

In simple thermal equilibrium, more minority carriers than can normally exist are created by the minority carrier injection process. Thus we have the surplus of carriers falling back into empty states in the valence band. In the valence band, an electron will combine with a hole and both will disappear (in the electrical sense only). Then the N-type material is short one electron and the P-type material is short one hole in the vicinity of the junction. But, of course, the external DC supply is continuously providing more carriers. Since adding a hole to the P-type semiconductor is equivalent to removing an electron from the valence band, there is a flow of electrons from the negative terminal, through the semiconductor device, and back to the power supply via the positive terminal.

Now that recombination is out of the way, we realize that a net flow of current is possible as a result of the injection-recombination process. And it is during recombination that light is produced. As said before, light production in a semiconductor solid-state light is called PN junction electroluminescence or injection luminescence.

Recombination

Basically, as an electron falls from the bottom of the conduction band and "recombines" with a hole at the top of the valence band, the electron gives up energy corresponding to the width of the forbidden gap. This energy is a direct result of the excitation by the external DC power source, which pumped or injected electrons to the higher energy state.

Since energy released is proportional to the forbidden gap width, it may be in the form of thermal energy (phonons) or of light quanta (photons). In the case of light quanta, the wavelength is determined by the difference in energy between the conduction and valence bands.

Consider Fig. 1-13. We see pictorially the process that involves energy changes at the PN junction during excitation.

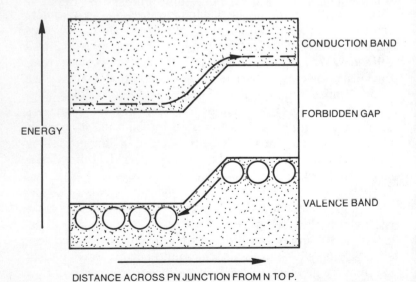

DISTANCE ACROSS PN JUNCTION FROM N TO P.

Fig. 1-13. Energy changes during excitation.

The electrons (-) cross the junction and increase in energy, while the holes cross the barrier in the opposite direction and lose energy. The region where the electrons are found is the conduction band and the region where the holes are found is called the valence band. Notice that electrons and holes don't change bands when crossing the PN junction, but merely change energy states within their respective bands.

Figure 1-14 shows the different possible methods of light quanta production. A solid line represents expelled heat while a dotted line is expelled light. In Fig. 1-14A we have recombination taking three steps as an electron is captured by a donor level and a hole is captured by an acceptor level. Donor-acceptor recombination then occurs. In this process, known as *radiative recombination*, both phonons and photons are emitted.

In Fig. 1-14B, band-to-band radiative emission is shown, in which no capture is evident. In C and D, light and heat are emitted because any donor or acceptor atoms present in the crystal lie at discrete levels in the forbidden gap. An electron in the process of changing energy levels may be temporarily trapped at one of these levels. To complete recombination, the electron now at this discrete level can recombine with a valence-band hole.

Returning to Fig. 1-14A, this process of radiative recombination is the most prevalent in the generation of light quanta in semiconductors. It should be easier to understand the idea of injection electroluminescence now. Electrons and holes are injected into the PN junction region by the application of an electric field supplied by the external DC supply. As the electrons and holes combine in the junction region, energy is released, resulting in luminescence, (light generation by radiative recombination).

If the current through the LED is varied, the light output will vary proportionately; that is, if the current is increased, the light output will increase. If we examine Fig. 1-12, we can notice certain characteristics of the solid-state lamp. The point where the current rises in the forward-bias direction is where light is first generated. In the reverse-bias condition, where the current suddenly flows, a situation called *breakdown* occurs. Here, light may also be generated by a method called *impact ionization*. This mechanism is inefficient and can cause complete destruction of the LED by overheating.

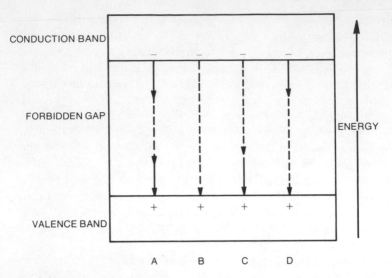

CONDUCTION BAND

FORBIDDEN GAP

ENERGY

VALENCE BAND

A   B   C   D

Fig. 1-14. Different modes of photon generation may include the production of phonons.

Figure 1-15 shows the emission of light from a semiconductor PN junction. Light is emitted at the junction and emanates in all directions. But since these emanations are usually blocked by the face of the crystal (they are light opaque), quanta leave the edges only.

Efficiency

We have stated that the process in Fig. 1-14A is the most common mechanism of light production. But this does not mean that it is the most efficient. Actually, Fig. 1-14B is the most intrinsically efficient light producer. This process takes place in *direct gap* semiconductor materials, and this simple band-to-band recombination conserves both energy and momentum. Multistep recombination processes can occur in direct-gap materials as well. The *indirect gap* materials do not conserve momentum during recombination; therefore, a unit of thermal energy (phonon) is emitted or absorbed in order that the overall momentum of the system be conserved. Direct-gap materials are used to produce laser emission.

To understand efficiency better, we can discuss different aspects of approach. *Internal quantum efficiency* is defined as the ratio of photons being generated at the junction to the electrons passing through the junction. In equation form, we would say:

$$Q.E. = \frac{\text{number of photons}}{\text{number of electrons}}$$

At very low temperature, the Q.E. of direct materials may approach 100%. In an indirect material, the electrons are trapped in different levels causing phonons to be generated as well as photons. Because of this indirect path from conduction band to valence band, the Q.E. for indirect materials is usually considerably lower than that of direct materials. In lasers the probability of a direct material producing laser action is considerably higher than an indirect material.

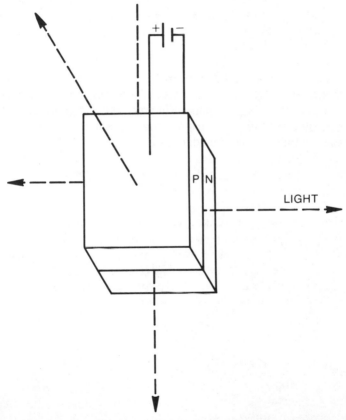

Fig. 1-15. Light is generated at the PN junction and is emanated in all directions.

Internal efficiency is also dependent on the purity of materials and process controls as well as the efficiency of the material. Internal absorption is primarily a characteristic of the transparency or opaqueness of the material. Since the majority of semiconductor materials have a high index of refraction, a large percentage of the photons are reflected back from the surface of the crystal. In this case the photons may travel across the crystal several times before they are emanated; they thus suffer a large reabsorption. These losses can be controlled by increasing the photon escape probability at the crystal's surface by shaping the diode properly or by proper encapsulation methods.

Other losses encountered are due to the electrical resistance of the contacts to the semiconductor crystal. These losses result in some degree of $I^2 R$ localized effects. Of course, there are other losses through optical effects such as absorptions, reflections, dispersion, and other effects due to the type of encapsulation used, lenses (if any), and the type of mount in use.

Looking into different materials for high internal efficiency is shadowed by the fact that not all semiconductors can be readily made into both N-type and P-type materials. Unfortunately, some semiconductor crystals are also unstable under ordinary non-laboratory conditions. Materials that perform satisfactorily in the lab many be unstable at normal temperatures, atmospheric conditions, or humidity.

Spectral Output

The last topic we need to cover before entering the realm of semiconductor light sources is that of spectral output. We would do best by returning to mathematics here and using formulas to describe these parameters.

The general equation for finding the wavelength of a radiative emission is

$$\lambda = hc/E$$

where λ = wavelength of radiation (microns)
h = Planck's constant (6.63×10^{-34} joule-seconds)
c = velocity of light in a vacuum (3×10^{14} microns/second)
E = energy (joules)

If we convert energy E from joules into electron-volts by the proper conversion, we can write

$$\lambda = 1.237/E_W$$

where 1.237 is equal to hc, and E_W is the energy bandwidth in electron-volts. (Energy bandwidth is defined as the difference between donor and acceptor levels.)

In the last two equations, the unit *micron* was used, which is equal to 10^3 nonometers (nm) or to 10^4 angstroms. The symbol for a micron is the Greek letter μ, and this unit should be remembered as it is one of the most commonly used units for wavelength measurement. In optics the preferred symbol for a micron is μm, which stands for a millionth of a meter, but in physics the symbol μ is usually satisfactory.

This about covers the basic theory of radiation emission in terms of the general terminology. A more comprehensive explanation concerning LEDs is given in Chapter 9, which includes technical and design information related to various commercially available units. It should be pointed out, though, that the material presented in Chapter 9 is not essential to the construction of the projects presented in this book, but rather is included for readers interested in designing new circuits from scratch.

PHOTOCELLS

As long as we are discussing photosensitive devices, it is well worth describing the properties of the photocell, one of the first semiconductor devices invented. Because of their low cost and relative simplicity, they still play a significant role in today's electronics. They are found in most light meters and are widely used in cameras with "electronic eyes."

Photocells are really *photoconductive* cells and are important optoelectronic devices. They are usually made of cadmium sulphide (CdS) or cadmium selenide (CdSe). Unlike the family of junction type photosensors, the photoconductive cell possesses no semiconductor junction. Instead, an entire layer of semiconductor material comprising the photocell changes resistance (Fig. 1-16). As the light level increases, this resistance decreases.

The "absolute" value of the resistance of a particular cell at a specific light level depends on many contributing factors—the photosensitive material being used for the cell

Fig. 1-16. Photocells are photoconductors whose resistances vary with the amount of light striking them.

fabrication, the cell size, electrode geometry, and of course the spectral composition of the incident light.

All photoconductive cells require an external power supply because they do not generate a photocurrent. This disadvantage is made up by the distinct advantage of having a sensitivity that is approximately 1000 times greater than photovoltaic cells, which do generate a photocurrent in response to incident light.

The photoconductive cell actually has a sensitivity about one million times greater in respect to constant (steady-state) light levels. Photodiodes and phototransistors have greater or faster response times than CdS or CdSe, but their poor sensitivity to such light levels limits their use to applications where relatively high illumination levels are encountered.

The sensitivity of the photoconductive cell depends on the wavelength of the incident light. Each photoconductive material has a unique response curve that indicates the portion of the light spectrum it is sensitive to. The CdS material has a peak response at 5500 angstroms, while CdSe has its peak at 7200 angstroms. In most applications, monochromatic light sources are not used. Instead, sunlight, a neon glow tube, or an incandescent source is used.

The overall response of a detector to a *continuous-spectrum* light source is *very* important in some applications. A photoconductive material should ideally have a flat response in respect to color temperature if it is to be used in continuous-spectrum applications. But applications where the cell is subjected to high, stray, ambient conditions, where the ambient radiation differs in color temperature from the signal source, requires that the cell's response be tailored to the wavelength of the source. For example, where the signal source is a tungsten incandescent lamp, and the stray ambient is a fluorescent lamp, the best choice would be a CdSe photoconductive cell. The problem is resolved because the sensitivity of the CdSe is suited to the tungsten spectrum since its peak response is towards the lower color temperature of this type of light source.

A perfectly linear photoconductive material is one in which a given percentage change in light level will produce the same percentage change in the resistance over the entire range of illumination. In general, CdSe cells are extremely linear below 1 footcandle and become nonlinear above as their sensitivity decreases. All CdS/CdSe photoconductors become less linear as the light level is increased until in the 10^5 fc range they are almost asymptotic.

In common with all types of photodetectors, photoconductors exhibit a phenomenon that has been called *fatigue*—also termed as *hysteresis* and *light memory*. The *instantaneous* conductance of a cell at a specific light level is a function of the cell's previous exposure to light and the duration of that exposure. The magnitude of this effect depends on the instantaneous light level, on the difference between the instantaneous and the previous light level, and the duration of the instantaneous and the previous exposures. The direction of this effect depends on whether the previous level was higher or lower than the instantaneous level.

A cell kept at a given "test" light level will attain an equilibrium conductance. If this same cell is kept at a lower level or in total darkness for some time and then checked at the test level, its conductance will be greater (relative to the equilibrium level) and will decay asymptotically to the equilibrium level. If the cell is kept at a higher light level and then measured at the test level, the initial conductance will be lower and will rise asymptotically to the equilibrium level. The magnitude of this effect is larger for CdSe than CdS cells, but the CdSe type of photoconductive cell tends to reach equilibrium more rapidly.

FIBER OPTICS

The principles behind transmission of light through a fiber-optic guide is generally accepted to be a wave

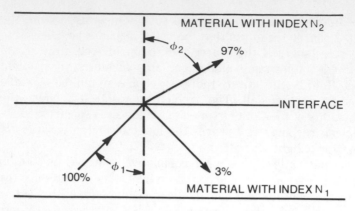

Fig. 1-17. Simple refraction happens to the ray of light as it passes through the interface of two materials having different indexes of refraction.

phenomenon. At visible frequencies the fibers of the "light pipe" actually acts as a wave guide for the electromagnetic radiation. For simplicity in the following discussion, standard, geometric, optical action will be considered to hold true for fiber-optic transmission. Total *internal* reflection is the underlying principle behind the transmission theories involved.

Refraction occurs whenever light passes from one material to another, and this action takes place because light tends to travel at different fixed velocities in different materials. According to Snell's law, a light beam traveling through one material with a refractive index of n_1 and at an angle of incidence ϕ_1 is bent (refracted) as it crosses the interface into another material whose index of refraction is n_2 at an angle ϕ_2. The equation for this operation is

$$n_1 \sin(\phi_1) = n_2 \sin(\phi_2)$$

This situation is shown in Fig. 1-17. The angle ϕ is always measured with respect to a perpendicular to the interface of the two materials. The direction of travel of the ray of light should be able to be reversed without changing the actual path the ray took.

For Snell's equation to be exact, the ray of light should be monochromatic in nature. A ray of light traveling through an optically dense material of index n_1 to a material that is optically rare of index n_2 crosses the interface and enters material 2 only if the angle of incidence ϕ_1 is less than the

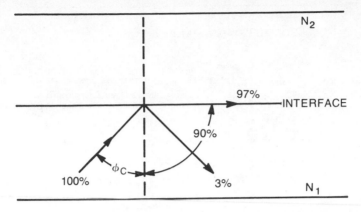

Fig. 1-18. The critical angle determines whether a ray of light will refract or not.

critical angle ϕ_C. At angles greater than ϕ_C, the light cannot cross the interface, and instead is totally reflected back into the first medium. In Figs. 1-18 and 1-19 we have light being refracted in the first diagram and totally reflected in the second. The critical angle, calculated from Snell's law, is

$$\sin(\phi_C) = n_1 / n_2$$

Since even the best silvered surface absorbs some of the incident light, prisms are used in quality optical instruments. The theory behind total internal reflection is also at work in glass prisms. With this type of reflection, almost no loss is

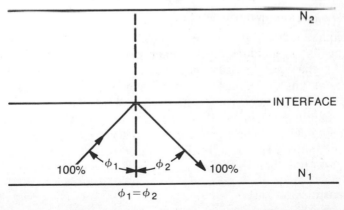

Fig. 1-19. Total internal reflection occurs when the angle of incidence is less than the critical angle.

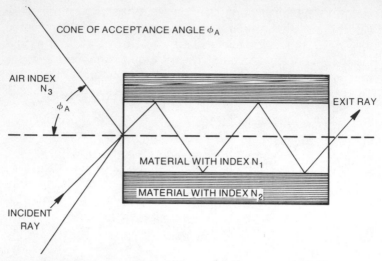

CONE OF ACCEPTANCE ANGLE ϕ_A

AIR INDEX
N_3

ϕ_A

EXIT RAY

MATERIAL WITH INDEX N_1

MATERIAL WITH INDEX N_2

INCIDENT
RAY

Fig. 1-20. A ray of light is transmitted through the "optic pipe" by total internal reflections that prevent light from escaping through the walls of the optic fiber.

encountered through the prism. To apply this theory to a fiber-optic light guide, a cylindrical core of glass with an index n_1 is clad with a second glass that has an index of refraction n_2. For total internal reflection to occur, n_1 must be greater than n_2 and the light ray to enter the fiber optic must be incident within the angle of acceptance ϕ_A. This angle is found from the formula

$$\sin(\phi_A) = \sqrt{n_1^2 - n_2^2}/n_3$$

This angle is also called the numerical aperture, usually designated N.A., and is the maximum angle at which a ray of light that is incident on the inner glass core can be trapped within the core. Any rays of light that are incident to the fiber core at angles beyond that represented by N.A. are either reflected or pass through the core-clad interface. Obviously, the capture power of the core increases as the maximum acceptance angle increases. In Fig. 1-20 you can see the course of a captured ray of light that entered within the acceptance angle of the fiber-optic core.

Transmission Losses

There are always some losses during transmission of the ray of light through the core. These losses depend on several factors. The absorption coefficient of the fiber-optic core determines how much the light ray will be attenuated throughout the length of the fiber. The average absorption loss for the latest experimental fibers is approximately 20% per mile for wavelengths between 4.5×10^{-5} and 10.0×10^{-5} cm. To transmit ultraviolet radiation, special cores have been developed.

Another area were losses occur are at the ends of the fiber optics. A single unclad rod, such as the material Lucite, can be employed to transmit light energy, but the transmission is quite poor at best. The smoothness and purity of the reflecting surface are the keys to efficient light transmission. With unclad single rods, there is a tendency for dirt to accumulate on or scratch the delicate outer surface. Another problem when using bundles of unclad fibers is the possibility that light will jump from fiber to fiber. This action will seriously degrade the performance of the optic guide.

The single fiber does have its uses, one of the most important being in the field of medicine. Here the single fiber is used in the fiber-optic laser system. The technique used is called *photocoagulation*, and is used to treat detached retinas in the eye. A portion of the laser fiber is excited, usually with a high-intensity flashtube. The output energy then travels down the single 300-micron diameter laser fiber to a handheld probe. The probe directs the tremendous energy to the desired spot on the retina.

The greatest uses of the fiber-optic guide is in bundles of clad fibers. These fibers are quite often used to transmit light energy to inaccessible areas and to pick up radiant information from these hard-to-get-at areas. Fiber optics are also used to a great extent in photosensitive circuits. If the ends of the bundles are fabricated in the exact same orientation to each other, you get a *coherent* bundle that will carry an image along its length. The possible uses of the "light pipe" go on and on almost without ending. For example, two guides may be used together, one carrying light as the source and the other being a coherent bundle. This arrangement allows observation into areas where it is normally not possible, as in making internal examinations of the stomach or lungs.

When experimenting, you can use relatively inexpensive fiber-optic tubes and bundles like those used in making decorative lamps. The higher attenuation losses of these inexpensive fibers are generally acceptable because of the shorter distances that the light or infrared signals will have to travel in most experiments. Also, such fibers are not critical about the wavelengths used. Only high-quality, low-loss fibers can be used for transmitting signals over great distances (several miles), and care must be taken to carefully match the wavelengths of the source and fiber for minimum attenuation.

Chapter 2

The Light-Emitting Diode

As we have seen in Chapter 1, the light-emitting diode or LED is basically a PN junction that will emit visible radiation, or nonvisible when forward biased. The material used in the construction of the more commonly available LEDs is gallium arsenide phosphide (GaAsP), which is a complex chemical substance derived from the elements gallium, arsenic, and phosporus. Typically, the (GaAsP) LED's output is in the wavelength region of 670 nanometers, which to the human eye is perceived as the color red. Of course, LEDs are made from compounds other than GaAsP, but to date the most common are the gallium arsenide phosphide types.

Figure 2-1 shows different LED light sources in comparison with the vision of the human eye and with the "vision" or, more appropriately, the sensitivity of silicon photosensor devices. Also, the curve for a standard tungsten filament lamp is included to give an idea of the different emission regions. Notice carefully that the LED sources are restricted and are relatively narrow in bandwidth, while the tungsten source is extremely broad. Also notice where the maximum output of the tungsten lamp occurs—at a point where the human eye has no sensitivity at all.

To help here and in other places through this book, a sensitivity curve for the human eye is shown in Fig. 2-2. To enable comparisons to be made, it is both greatly expanded and is calibrated in relative response and lumens/watt.

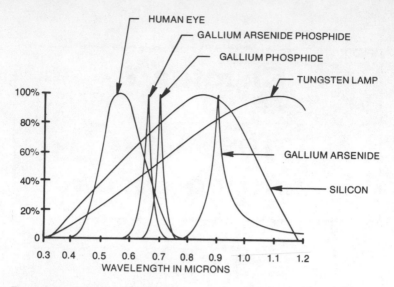

Fig. 2-1. Spectra of the tungsten lamp and several LED compounds compared with the response of silicon and the human eye.

The characteristics of various LEDs are given in Table 2-1. Many more types exist, but we will use these for a basis to begin with. These characteristics differ in many respects, yet they do possess parameters that are similiar in nature.

LEDs in general are low-heat-generating devices. The cliche "cold light" does apply here, especially if you compare the thermal output of a solid-state lamp with that of a tungsten lamp. Figure 2-3 shows the typical curve of a tungsten lamp with a temperature (color temperature) of 2850°K. Notice that most of its output energy is in the nonvisible portions of the electromagnetic spectrum. Human vision extends roughly from 0.360μ to 0.760μ. The tungsten lamp's greatest output occurs at 1.1μ, and not only that but it extends deeply into the infrared region. It can almost be said that the tungsten lamp is as good, if not better, a thermal source than a light source. Also notice that its energy output is extremely broad and not contained. Why do we mention this point? Because a perfect light source in essence should be a light source, not a thermal source. Of course, the reason that the tunsten lamp is a good thermal source is that it is an *incandescent* lamp and uses the heating effect of an electric current through its filament.

This brings up other advantages of the solid-state lamp. A filament must be heated to a high temperature, but the

Table 2-1. Efficiency of LED

LED TYPE	COLOR	WAVELENGTH (microns)	EFFICIENCY	LUMENS/WATT (optical)	LUMENS/WATT (electrical)
GaAsP	yellow	0.585	—	500	—
GaAsP	red	0.660	0.03%	40	0.012
GaAsP	red	0.670	0.1%	20	0.02
GaAsP	orange	0.610	0.001%	330	0.003
GaP	green	0.565	0.01%	590	0.05
GaP	red	0.690	1%	15	0.15

filament will undergo chemical combination with the gases within the bulb of the lamp. The higher the operating temperature, the faster the combinations will occur, decreasing the life time of the bulb. In contrast, the LED enjoys a particularly long expected operating life of about

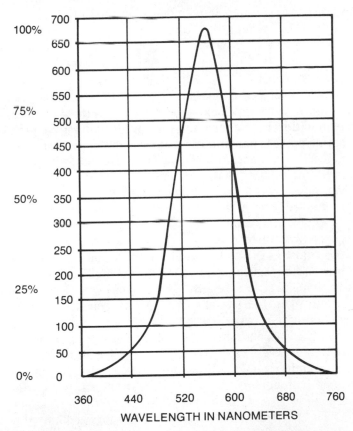

Fig. 2-2. Response of the human eye, given both as a percentage and in lumens per watt.

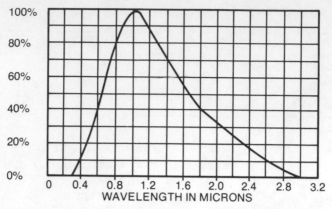

Fig. 2-3. Percentage output of a tungsten lamp at 2850°K.

100,000 hours. (Note: Some modern incandescent displays are completely evacuated and provide comparable life expectancies.)

Because the filament takes time to heat up, the tungsten lamp cannot be modulated very high in frequency, whereas the semiconductor light source can be modulated at frequencies above 100 kHz easily. The LED has a fast response with a rise time and a fall time measured in parts of a microsecond, this means that the response to an electric excitation will be quick (rise time) and also that the LED will extinguish its output almost immediately with the removal of the excitation energy. The filament lamp will continue to glow even after the current is removed since the filament must cool from its high operating temperature.

Needless to say, filament lamps are more fragile than LEDs. Most filament lamps also require some sort of holder, while the LED, because of its built-in strength, rarely requires any support. By strength, we mean here the structural strength. The LED has a very small weight, so the leads (contact wires) will generally support the light source. In some cases a positioner is used to keep the LED in position with reference to associated components. As far as compatibility goes, the low impedance of the solid-state lamp makes it ideal in conjunction with most semiconductor circuitry.

The light-emitting diode looks like a forward-biased diode with a breakdown voltage of approximately 1.6V, which indicates that a low-voltage power supply is required.

50

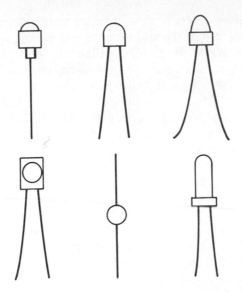

Fig. 2-4. LEDs come in a multitude of shapes and colors.

As LEDs are usually fabricated using a plastic or metal-plastic encapsulation, an LED can be made into various sizes and shapes as depicted in Fig. 2-4. Of course, LEDs are used not only as status indicators (light sources) but as readouts and light sources for detectors and monitors.

Where required, an LED can be fabricated with an output, not in the visible region, but in the infrared region of the electromagnetic spectrum. Such diodes are appropriately named *infrared emitters*. To the GaAs diode, a percentage of zinc is diffused, causing the gallium arsenide diode to emit radiation at 0.890μ. At this wavelength the radiation emitted is definitely not perceivable to the human eye, but is ideally matched with the spectral response of silicon photodetectors. Very useful characteristics appear in a system comprising of an infrared emitter and a silicon photodiode or phototransistor. These uses range from optically coupled isolators (OCI) to scanning devices.

As far as the tungsten filament goes, we can say that the incandescent light source is quite broad in spectral distribution and is generally acceptable for illumination purposes. The same statement applies also for standard fluorescent-type tubes, except that these illuminators tend to have spectral peaks in the visible spectrum, thereby tending to shift the colors of items viewed under their illumination. The output bandwidth of the solid-state lamp is contained to a few nanometers, while the tungsten filament lamp extends over 2700 nanometers, beginning in the deep infrared, peaking in the near infrared, and falling off throughout the visible spectrum and sharply in the near ultraviolet. If the temperature is shifted, the spectral response shifts accordingly. If the temperature is increased, the shift will result in more efficiency in the visible and ultraviolet regions and a decrease in the infrared, but the life expectance drops quickly with an increase in temperature.

Two old contenders against the LED are neon and argon glow lamps. The output of both vary directly with the current application. Typically, a neon glow tube will emit radiation at 0.52μ and 0.75μ. Some infrared radiation is also emitted as a band between 0.82μ and 0.88μ. The neon thus produces radiation at different areas in the electromagnetic spectrum. As an illuminant, the neon light source is practically useless because its efficiency is very low, usually around 0.06 lumens per milliampere for standard bulbs and increasing to 0.15 lumens/mA for high-output types. But, as an indicator light source, the neon is quite good, except that it has two drawbacks, one is voltage, the other is color.

Neon lamps operate as ionization devices, so a potential around 90 volts is required. This high potential usually requires an AC power supply instead of batteries, or if portability is required, the designer must either use an expensive high-voltage battery or else design an oscillator power supply (which is seldom inexpensive). Of course, direct interface with standard semiconductor circuits is difficult since the high voltage potentials encountered would certainly cause most device breakdown voltages to be exceeded. As far as the color is concerned, the spectral output is always a yellowish red or orange. Under normal conditions the neon light source has a life of about 25,000 hours. Here again, the solid-state lamp is easily in the lead.

Basically, LEDs are visible and infrared emitters. It is here that the argon-type glow tube excels. The argon lamp produces ultraviolet radiation in quantities great enough to be an ultraviolet (UV) energy source. But for this advantage the argon lamp pays a great premium—its useful life expectancy is about 1000 to 3000 hours, with its UV energy dropping to 50%

after 150 hours in ¼-watt bulbs and after 1000 hours in 2-watt lamps. The argon glow tube has an output of about 3.5 fluorens per watt.

Glow tubes, as said before, depend on the ionization of the gas trapped in the bulb. Ionization times in complete darkness are measured in fractions of a second, where the light or radiation output follows the current almost linearly up to approximately 15 kHz.

OPTICALLY COUPLED ISOLATORS

What about other uses for light-emitting diodes? Returning to the infrared emitters, let's take a deeper look into optically coupled isolators (OCI). Basically, an OCI consists of a gallium arsenide (GaAs) infrared light-emitting diode optically coupled to a silicon photodetector, such as a photodiode or phototransistor. This versatile system can switch off and on with speeds in the microsecond region. With this type of speed, information may be relayed anywhere from DC to hundreds of kilohertz. Since there is no electrical connection between the light source and the detector, the OCI will provide unidirection control with no feedback to the control. Actually, the isolation resistance between the energy source and the detector is often measured around 10^{11} ohms with a coupling capacitance of approximately 1 pF (10^{-12} farad). The efficiency of these units may be as high as 50%, sometimes even more, and the output is linear with respect to the input. Some of the uses for the OCI are as interfaces between transistors and integrated circuits, applications in memory units such as computer central processing units (CPUs) or in input/output (I/O) interfaces. If you regard the OCI as a discrete circuit element, it can replace the more commonly used relays and transformers. Comparing the OCI with relays, the OCI is much faster in operation, with an extremely positive action—no bounce.

Bounce is where a contact hops before it comes to rest. In certain applications such as in CPUs, this action can cause errors as the bounces produce erroneous information.

Relays are inherently sensitive to vibrations and shocks where the OCI is unbothered by either. Of course since there are no moving parts as in relays, there is a greater life expectancy. Relays tend to wear at their contacts, become pitted from current flow, and the springs suffer from metal

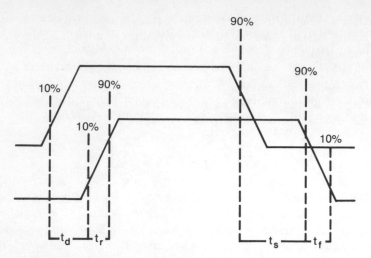

Fig. 2-5. Between the input and output of an optically coupled isolator there always exists a time lag.

fatigue. The OCI usually has a greater operating temperature range than a relay. They are also much smaller than a relay can be fabricated. As far as digital circuitry goes, the OCI is compatible both with DTL and TTL integrated circuits.

In comparison with transformers, the OCI has a frequency response from DC to hundreds of kilohertz. Because of its low coupling capacitance, there also exists better common-mode rejection. Here again, the OCI is smaller than transformers and, as with relays, the ordinary transformer is subject to damage from vibrations and shocks were the optically coupled isolator is not.

Since the optically coupled isolator is the one place where the LED has no rival, we will discuss the terminology involved with this interesting device. In trying to describe the operation of OCIs, we can make use of general transistor parameters as well as parameters specially suited to OCIs. Such specially suited parameters are coupling efficiency, input/output capacitance, current transfer ratio, and voltage isolation.

One of the most important parameters involved with OCIs is switching time. Since the LED section of the OCI switches in the nanosecond range (rise time), we can generally ignore the LED and regard the detector portion of the optically coupled isolator. Turning to Fig. 2-5 for a moment, let's discuss the two waveforms shown. The upper waveform is the applied signal to the LED terminals of the device, and the lower waveform is the output available at the photodetector terminals of the OCI. The following four parameters are the ones depicted by the two waveforms:

Delay Time (t_d)—the time measured from the application of a signal to the LED until current in the photodetector changes from zero to 10% of its full output.

Rise Time (t_r)—the time required for the current of the photodetector to change from 10% to 90% of its full output.

Storage Time (t_s)—the time measured between the removal of the applied signal and a point at which the photodetector's current is 90% of its full output.

Fall Time (t_f)—the time required for the photodetector's current to change from 90% to 10% of its full output.

In all cases, the term *full output* refers to the maximum final current present at the photodetector terminals of the OCI.

Phototransistors

Phototransistor operation depends on the effect that radiative illumination will have upon the semiconductor material the transistor comprises. This effect is, of course, called the photoelectric effect. If radiation of the proper wavelength illuminates the semiconductor, electron-hole pairs will be produced within the material. If a voltage is applied to the device, the carriers will move, causing a current flow. Since the current flow is proportional to the number of electron-hole pairs being created, the greater the intensity of the applied illuminance, the greater the current flow. It is in the region of the base-collector junction that the carrier production occurs in a phototransistor.

Take for an example an NPN-type phototransistor. Holes from the generated electron-hole pairs tend to gather in the base region of the transistor. Actually, holes produced in the base remain there, while holes generated in the collector region migrate into the base by the strong field at the junction. By the same process, electrons tend to accumulate in the collector. The net charge does not really change, but distributes itself through the regions involved. As a result, holes diffuse across the region of the base toward the base-emitter junction. As the holes reach the junction, they are injected into the emitter region of the transistor. This causes the emitter to pump electrons into the base. Since the efficiency of the emitter injection is greater than that of the base injection, for every injected hole, many electrons are pumped across the junction.

Toward the collector, the emitter-injected electrons flow through the base. At the collector, the injected electrons meet with the photogenerated electrons in the collector and produce the collector current. Since the collector-base region is the site of the actual photogenerated electrons, the greater the collector region is in the area, the more carriers that will be developed.

A phototransistor can be effectively converted into a photodiode by using only the base and collector terminals—the emitter terminal is left open. This operation will reduce sensitivity, but increases speed. Generally, photodiode operation is useful in digital applications while phototransistor operation is used in analog work.

DISPLAYS

Another use for the combination of LEDs and photodetectors is in the fabrication of arrays. An LED array has several advantages over an array composed of tungsten filament lamps. Filaments tend to sag with age, causing numerous problems. Reliability is greatly increased with the use of the solid-state light-emitting diode. Of course, longer life also makes replacement of arrays less frequent with solid-state lamps. The LEDs structural stability and resistance against shocks and vibrations provide additional factors that increase the desirability of using solid-state devices. Because of the small area taken up by the LED "chip," a greater packing density can be achieved, with less interference from ambient extraneous light sources. As mentioned before, LED power requirements are much less than that required for a filament type of light source. Add the compatibility with integrated circuits and the low thermal energy output of solid-state lamps, and we find that the LED is again in the lead.

The LED is not a newcomer to displays, nor is it alone. Displays, both numeric and alphabetic, have been around for quite while. But it is the light-emitting diode that gave the final push to make digital displays acceptable in all areas of interest. Because of their small size, low power consumption, single-plane readout, and digital IC compatibility, portable

Fig. 2-6. Seven-segment readouts can be made in a variety of sizes. This Monsanto unit is 0.37-inch high and is comparable in size to a postage stamp. The display uses plastic diffusers to increase the size of the individual segments driven by the small LED light sources inside.

equipment that could have never existed is now found everywhere.

LEDs turn on and off with great speed, so multiplexing techniques can be applied to a series of display elements, thus cutting down the number of driving components required in a given system. The seven-segment LED display is now commonly found in digital voltmeters, watches, and other types of equipment requiring a digital readout. One place where the LED seven-segment readout is familiar to everyone is the calculators being manufactured by many major companies in electronics. Figures 2-6 and 2-7 show typical light-emitting seven-segment displays.

The other rivals of the LED display are the gas discharge tube, the fluorescent display, the liquid crystal display, and the filament display. The fluorescent display provides a blue-green light and may come in a large 9-pin tube with a single digit or a multidigit tube as found in many imported calculators. Basically, where the LED and other displays are light *sources*, the liquid crystal display (LCD) is a light *controller*; that is, it can control the passage of light. (The LCD is such an important device that we will spend a separate chapter on it.)

Fig. 2-7. Multidigit displays in the 12-digit array shown above are incorporated into many calculators. The Hewlett-Packard HP-21 scientific calculator uses this 12-digit array to display 10 numerals and 2 minus signs. Each 7-segment digit has its own magnifying lens to make the displayed character look about twice as large.

Returning to LED displays, the seven-segment display uses either common-cathode or common-anode connection techniques. LED displays fabricated by the monolithic (single chip) process are only of the common cathode type. Hybrid

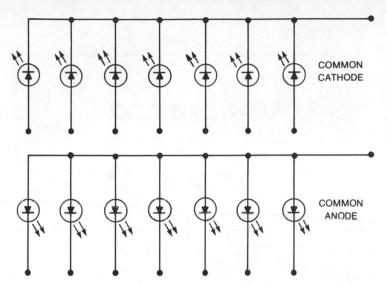

Fig. 2-8. LED 7-segment readouts are manufactured in common-cathode and common-anode configurations.

technology using discrete LED chips can produce either type. Figure 2-8 shows the internal structure connections for common-anode and common-cathode displays.

Chapter 3

The LED In Use

Before going any deeper into displays and photodetectors let's explore the realm of the light-emitting diode. The use of LEDs goes further than just a pretty little light. As on-board status indicators in circuit cards in computers, literally millions of man-hours have been saved. If a problem develops on a certain board, a light-emitting diode lights up, indicating a fault. Filament lights are not practical from many view points, and some of these points also apply to neon glow tubes.

LEDs require approximately 1.6V of forward bias before they conduct (turn on). It is rather easy to design circuits to take advantage of this built-in switching mechanism. With a filament lamp, current flows continuously, so a more elaborate circuit is required. This is not to say that some LED status indicator circuits are not sophisticated. Actually, some LED circuits are very sophisticated. But for status and indicators in general, this level of construction is not required. For example, suppose that if a voltage drop occurs this is indicative of a transistor failure. The designer of the circuit could build a digital voltmeter on the card that would read the voltage drop and display it on an LED readout, but this is not practical. In most cases such a status indicator would represent a higher cost than the circuit it is keeping tabs on.

The primary drawback of using a neon lamp as an indicator is that a neon glow tube needs about 90V before it will ionize and glow. The neon glow tube does have a built-in switch, so to speak, like the LED, but the voltage requirements of the neon are not consistent with that of typical transistor or integrated circuit supplies. Besides, both the neon and the filament represent a greater power consumption in their operation. The LED takes up little space because of its small size. Another point to remember is that the life span of a light-emitting diode is much greater than that of a filament or glow lamp.

In much equipment, if not most, an indicator is present to signify whether or not power is present. Here again we can see why the solid-state lamp is better. First, it requires very little power. Second, it can be operated at most voltage potentials if the proper current-limiting resistor is used. Third, it will require replacement less often, if at all, since in most cases it will exceed the life span of the equipment it is associated with. LEDs are also available in green, red, yellow, amber, orange, and even blue.

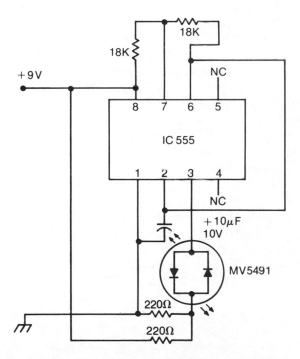

Fig. 3-1. A specially prepared two-color LED makes this novel flasher possible.

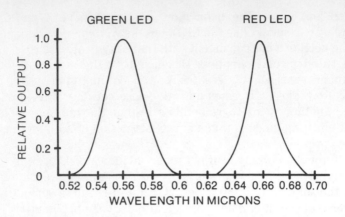

Fig. 3-2. Spectral distribution for the MV5491 LED. (Courtesy Monsanto.)

LED STATUS INDICATORS

A flashing light is always an attention getter, whether it be in a toy or an indicator that signals that a problem exists on a million-dollar computer. Figure 3-1 shows a rather simple circuit using one timing IC (Signetics 555), four resistors, and one capacitor. The circuit will flash a special two-color LED made by Monsanto, which is actually two LEDs in one package, each connected in the opposite direction—one LED is red and the other is green. This circuit not only turns current on and off, but reverses the polarity of the current flow. Thus, we have a circuit that alternately flashes green and red, using only one solid-state lamp. Figure 3-2 shows the spectral distribution for the two halves of the diode.

Of course, this same two-color LED can also be incorporated into a very simple circuit to indicate current direction, with one color indicating one direction and the second color indicating the other, thereby making a polarity indicator. Figure 3-3 shows such a simple polarity indicator. This particular circuit is designed for testing polarity with ±5V supplies when working with digital integrated circuits. Most digital circuits use a nominal +5V power supply, so this circuit will allow testing for voltage polarity before hooking up a circuit. The red portion of this LED is a GaAsP type, while the green half is a GaP.

We talked before about using an LED as an on-indicator. Here again we can see a simple but interesting circuit in Fig. 3-4. The LED being used is capable of being operated from

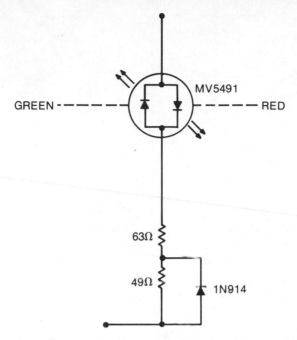

Fig. 3-3. Simple polarity indicator for 5-volt signals. The two resistors and 1N914 diode were chosen to produce green and red colors of equal brightness. Since the GaAsP and GaP diodes have different efficiencios, the 0.7V voltage drop of the 1N914 must be taken into account when selecting resistor values in other circuits.

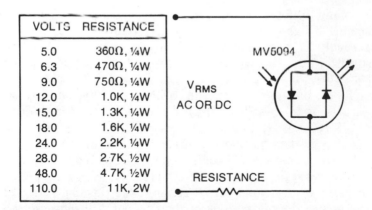

VOLTS	RESISTANCE
5.0	360Ω, ¼W
6.3	470Ω, ¼W
9.0	750Ω, ¼W
12.0	1.0K, ¼W
15.0	1.3K, ¼W
18.0	1.6K, ¼W
24.0	2.2K, ¼W
28.0	2.7K, ½W
48.0	4.7K, ½W
110.0	11K, 2W

Fig. 3-4. An LED indicator for both AC and DC operation. The resistance is selected for the operating voltage desired. The values listed above are for a forward current $I_F = 10$ mA, assuming an LED forward voltage drop $V_F = 1.56V$. For other voltage values, $R = (V_{RMS} - V_F)/I_F$.

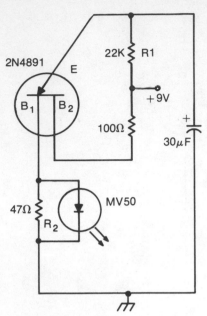

Fig. 3-5. UJT relaxation oscillator.

either direct or alternating current. The input voltage can range from 5.0V to 110.0V, depending on the current-limiting resistor used. The table in the figure gives different resistor values, depending on the applied voltage. The color of this solid-state lamp is red, with a peak output in its spectral distribution at 0.66μ.

Many different approaches can be tried in regard to flashing a light-emitting diode at different frequencies. Two relatively simple methods involve using a unijunction transistor or its cousin, the programmable unijunction transistor. In Fig. 3-5, a unijunction (UJT) relaxation oscillator has as its load an LED. Basically, the circuit operates as follows: The 30 μF capacitor is charged through the 22K resistor (R_1) by the power supply, which is 9V DC. The capacitor is then discharged through R_2 and the LED by the UJT. The flashing rate is controlled by the applied voltage and the time constant of the capacitor and R_1. By increasing either the value of the capacitor or resistor, the flashing rate will slow down; decreasing one of their values will increase the rate.

A second unijunction flasher circuit (Fig. 3-6) uses a special form of unijunction, called the programmable unijunction transistor (PUT). This circuit operates similarly to the UJT relaxation oscillator. The 2 μF capacitor discharges periodically through the LED as the PUT goes to the *on* state. In this circuit, the components are a little more critical than in the UJT oscillator. Here the ratio between the 3.9K resistor and the 22K resistor may have to be adjusted for optimum performance.

Special Devices

Recently, there has been talk of a special light-emitting diode that has the unique feature of changing its color, depending on the applied voltage. One such diode is manufactured by Electronics Unlimited, and the LED is called an MV1. The color changes and voltage potential are given in the following table, but keep in mind that these figures only apply when a 47Ω current-limiting resistor is used.

Red: 1.6 to 4.0V
Orange: 4.0 to 5.5V
Yellow: 5.5 to 9.0V
Chartreuse: 9.0 to 12V
Green: 12 to 15.0V

The exact voltage potential required for the MV1 LED to change colors may vary slightly from diode to diode. Thus, if the application requires precision, it may be necessary to calibrate the LED before using it.

In observing the circuits so far, you've probably noticed that in almost every case where an LED is used, a

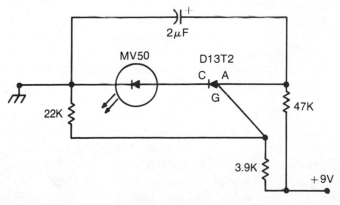

Fig. 3-6. PUT flasher.

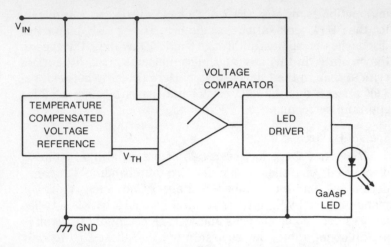

Fig. 3-7. Block diagram of HP 5082-4732.

current-limiting resistor is needed. This series resistor is required as LEDs are *very* current sensitive and can be easily burned out. The series resistor can also be used to control the brightness of the LED; depending on its value, different forward currents will result. When using any LED or, any other semiconductor, always check with its specification sheet to determine its various maximum ratings.

Discussing series resistors, it should be mentioned here that Hewlett Packard has two interesting lines of special LEDs. The first has an integral resistor incorporated in the housing, making an external series resistor unnecessary. The second series is highly sophisticated; it actually contains a voltage-sensing IC in the encapsulation. These latter LEDs are ideal as battery-level indicators in portable equipment, logic level indicators in digital circuitry, and literally hundreds of other applications where the voltage level (or current) is important. The internal structure looks somewhat like Fig. 3-7 and would operate as such. The GaAsP LED turns on when input voltage V_{IN} exceeds threshold voltage V_{TH}. The built-in voltage comparator with its high gain provides unambiguous indications. For detecting current levels, the unit can be connected in parallel with a resistor such that the voltage drop across the resistor equals the threshold voltage at the proper current level. For higher voltage levels, the unit can be connected across a resistor in a voltage divider to vary the effective input voltage.

LED PULSE AND MODULATOR CIRCUITS

We stated earlier that LEDs can be modulated at very high frequencies. The following circuit will modulate common light-emitting diodes at frequencies up to 10 MHz. If special GaAs LEDs are used, the modulating frequency can be raised to 100 MHz. High-frequency transistors are used in Fig. 3-8, but if you are simply interested in modulation at lower frequencies, the choice of transistors becomes much more broad.

The modulator circuit could be used, for example, with the appropriate receiver to transmit RF signals over a light beam. Here, as in most communications applications, the choice of an IR (infrared radiation) emitting diode is usually better. The IR units are generally more efficient and have better transmission characteristics through air.

In Fig. 3-9, an LED is being driven from an avalanche transistor. This circuit provides a pulse of radiation with a duration in the nanosecond range. The rise time is less than 10^{-8} seconds. If an IR light-emitting diode is used, the output will be only a few milliwatts but with a pulse repetition rate of a few kilohertz. This type of circuit has application where a pulsing radiant-energy source is required with a pulse duration that is very brief.

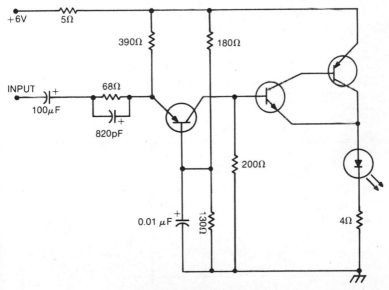

Fig. 3-8. LED modulator.

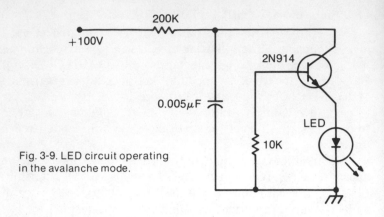

Fig. 3-9. LED circuit operating
in the avalanche mode.

The next circuit (Fig. 3-10) is one of the simplest in this book and is the most common configuration used in power indicators. This circuit was designed to operate from the normal 120V AC line voltage. The 0.47 μF capacitor limits dissipation in the circuit elements to 200 mW or less. The circuit is self-protecting with respect to line-voltage spikes and transients. Approximately 10 mA of current is drawn by the elements in this indicator circuit.

LED/PHOTOTRANSISTOR CIRCUITS

Earlier we mentioned that LEDs have found their way into computers via two methods—trouble indicators and status indicators. Let's stop for a moment and consider the ways light-emitting diodes can be put to use in these two roles. First, let's take a peek at different logic circuits to see how LEDs would fit in.

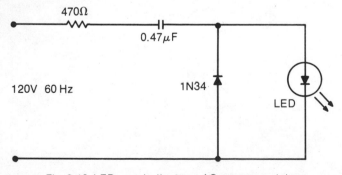

Fig. 3-10. LEDs can indicate an AC power-on status.

68

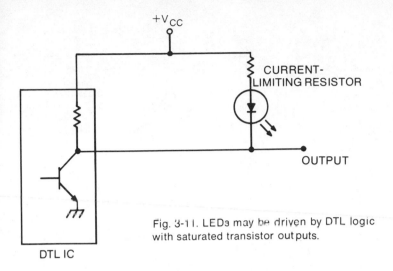

Fig. 3-11. LEDs may be driven by DTL logic with saturated transistor outputs.

DTL IC

Logic Circuits

The output of most diode/transistor logic (DTL) circuits is in the form of a saturated transistor driver. The transistor would normally be driving a pullup resistor, so the most practical way of introducing an LED would be in the fashion shown in Fig. 3-11. A factor that is important when considering an LED as a load on a DTL integrated circuit is the total resistance of the DTL load and the LED. Also remember that a series resistor is required with the LED.

A more common use in digital circuitry for LEDs is that of transistor/transistor logic (TTL) register status indicators (Fig. 3-12). Here again, the loading must be watched. Before

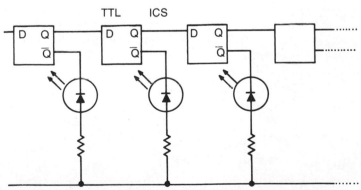

Fig. 3-12. LEDs may be used as register status indicators.

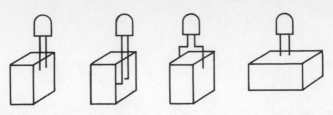

Fig. 3-13. LEDs may be mounted in a variety of ways on a printed-circuit board.

connecting any LED up to an IC, check whether the integrated circuit has sufficient current-handling capacity. And check whether the voltage present at the IC's output is high enough to light the diode. As stated before, most light-emitting diodes require approximately 1.6V of forward bias before they will emit radiation.

Figure 3-13 shows typical on-card mountings for LEDs. LEDs are usually mounted on the edge of the card to facilitate viewing them, since most computer cards are fitted edgewise into electrical card connectors. Of course, LEDs are also used on the control console of computers as status indicators.

Card Reader

Most computers do not use punched cards as much as they used to, but even those that do are enjoying a more modern approach. Before, several different methods were used to read the punched cards. Most common was the reader that had a metallic surface on one side and a series of sensor wires on the other. As the punched-out holes passed under the sensor, the wire would contact the metallic surface and a circuit would be formed. These readers were slow, required maintenance continuously, and were prone to errors. An optical system is the answer, and with the use of IR emitters even the need for closing off ambient light is removed. On one side of the card are IR-emitting LEDs, and on the other, IR-sensitive detectors. The IR detectors are suitably protected with a deep red filter (designed to pass IR only) so they will produce errors by varying ambient light sources. Figure 3-14 is a possible arrangement for such a card reader.

Counter

While we are on the subject of IR emitters, it is obvious that they are the ideal choice when ambient light surrounds

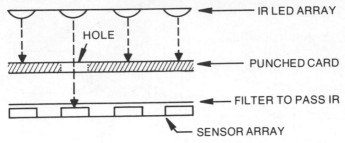

Fig. 3-14. A solid-state card reader.

the emitter and detector. For example, an IR LED and sensor can make up a *hole or event* counter as in Fig. 3-15. Here, the circuit may be designed to count missing objects or materials or, of course, count the opposite—those that *are* present.

In another application such as Fig. 3-16, the IR emitter is focused on a traveling plane surface, which is marked with reflective lines. Holes can also be cut in the plane surface and a reflective surface placed behind the traveling plane surface. The reflective marks could actually be objects on a moving conveyor belt, or they could be ink marks on a wire or ribbon. Marked objects moving down the belt could be counted by this easy method, and the ribbon or wire could measure predetermined intervals.

In measuring weights, a simple lever attachment to a balance could be used to block the irradiance from the IR LED to the sensor and turn off the load mechanism. The areas where LEDs are useful go on almost without end.

Warning Indicator

Figure 3-17 shows a rather simple warning indicator that will alternately flash one LED and then the other. The circuit

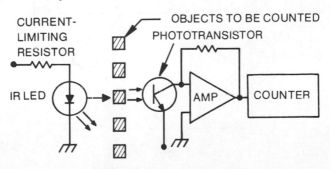

Fig. 3-15. A simple event counter.

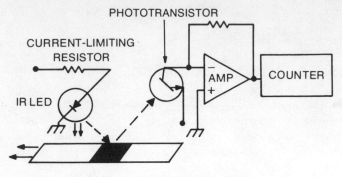

Fig. 3-16. A reflective type event counter.

is straightforward and almost any PNP transistors may be used for Q_1 and Q_2. I have used a 2N2901 and had excellent results. If you have NPN transistors, the same circuit can be used by merely switching around all DC polarities.

Logic Probe

Many different companies make devices called *logic status indicators* in which their main readout is an LED lamp.

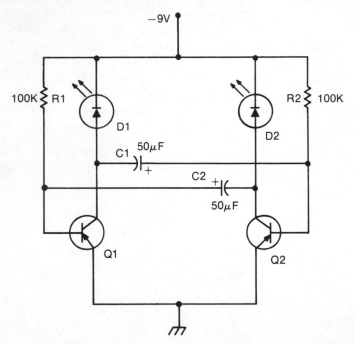

Fig. 3-17. Alternately flashing LED circuit for use as a warning indicator.

72

When checking digital circuitry, it is possible to use many different types of test equipment, such as multimeters, oscilloscopes, and other quite sophisticated test gear. But there is also a simpler and sometimes more practical way to test digital circuitry—with a logic probe.

Most digital circuitry depends on voltage levels, and one of these levels is called *1*, *on*, or *high*, and the other, *0*, *off*, or *low*. If we build a simple device that will light an LED when a 1 logic level is present and extinguish the LED when a 0 logic level is present, we can in most cases test to see if a given circuit or IC is operating properly and if the proper voltage levels are being fed to it.

Figure 3-18 shows a simple circuit that uses an N-type field-effect transistor (FET) as the amplifier and isolator. A low-level negative signal at the input creates an electric field in the FET that will block current flow through the device. If a low-level positive signal is applied instead, the electric field will disappear and allow current flow. With the passage of current through the FET the LED will light, thus indicating the presence of a positive signal (logic *1* or *on*).

The extremely high input impedance of this probe does not load down the outputs or inputs of digital circuitry. Loading can cause erratic behavior or possibly destruction of the IC being tested if too high a current flow is developed. In practice, the input resistor of this circuit can be increased in resistance value to 100 megohms and the circuit would still continue to operate properly. The 100Ω series resistor is usually included to limit current flow through the LED.

To use the logic probe, connect the circuit's negative battery terminal to the negative terminal of the power supply

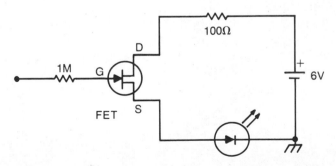

Fig. 3-18. A simple logic probe that uses an FET as an amplifier and isolator.

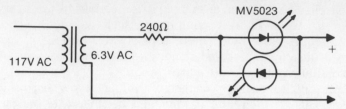

Fig. 3-19. LEDs can make a simple semiconductor go/no-go tester.

of the circuit being tested. Then touch the probe tip to the different leads of the ICs. If a manual is available for the circuitry involved, it will undoubtedly give a logic diagram for circuit operation. Using this logic diagram, it is possible to follow the various signal paths with the probe.

Transistor/Diode Tester

Another simple test circuit is shown in Fig. 3-19. The power supply applies alternating current to the two LEDs, so only one or the other will illuminate at a time. The two LEDs being in parallel will protect each other from reverse current flow during the half cycle that provides reverse polarity to one LED and forward polarity to the other. When a good diode or transistor is tested, current should flow in only one direction. Thus, only one LED should light. If one LED is lit brightly and the other very dimly while testing such an unidirectional device, the device is most likely not defective. But if both LEDs light up brightly, the device is probably shorted. Of course, if both are not lit, the device is considered to be open. By labeling the two LEDs, it can be readily established whether the device is conducting on the positive or negative portion of the cycle, making it possible to find diode cathodes and anodes and identify PNP and NPN transistors.

Resistors can be tested also, but the results are hard to interpret. As far as a continuity tester goes, however, this circuit is ideal. The less resistance encountered, the greater the glow from the LEDs. Even capacitors above 0.05 μF can be tested; if they are good, both LEDs should light up faintly.

Sound Movies

Before we leave the discussion of discrete LEDs, as opposed to use in arrays, one other interesting use has appeared for the LED. The motion picture industry has established a practice of placing the audio portion of a picture along a modulated strip on the film (see Fig. 3-20). Before the advent of LEDs, incandescent lamps were used to produce a beam of light which when passed through the strip on the film would be modulated. The beam would then be picked up by a light-sensitive device, demodulated, and amplified. Figure 3-21 shows a typical circuit where an LED has taken the place of the filament lamp as the source of light. Since the LED has a relatively tight beam (small divergence) and the spectral output is nearly monochromatic, the LED makes an appropriate device for this purpose. Later we will discuss long-distance transmission over a light beam.

OPTICALLY COUPLED ISOLATORS

An extremely interesting and important array is that of the optically coupled isolator, which usually contains one emitter and one detector. Optically coupled isolators (OCIs) are very useful where large common-mode signals are encountered, such as in the line receivers of digital circuits.

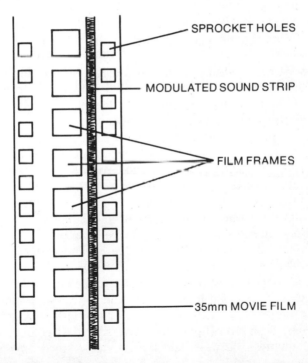

Fig. 3-20. The audio portion of a movie film modulates a carrier beam in the projector.

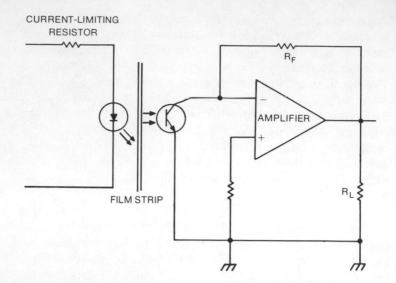

Fig. 3-21. Typical circuit used in projectors for sound pickup.

Logic isolation involved with digital work, telephone equipment, and medical applications also benefit from the use of OCIs.

In many instances, circuit designers are faced with problems of providing circuit isolation in order to prevent ground loops and common-mode signals. In the past, the typical electronic devices called upon to perform these tasks were line receivers, transformers, and relays. But transformers and relays are slow-speed devices by nature and are thus incompatible with modern logic circuits. Line receivers have the required speed, but are limited to about 3 volts in reference to common-mode signals. The line receiver also suffers from the problem of not supplying sufficient isolation; thus ground-loop signals develop.

Figure 3-22 shows the package style typical of OCIs. Figure 3-23 shows the internal structure of the more common varieties of optically coupled isolators. The basic structure of the OCI consists of a light-emitting diode optically connected to the input of a photosensitive device. The photosensitive device is some type of photosensitive silicon detector. There is no opaqueness between the two devices, since any optical impedance would result in a lowering of the transfer characteristics of the OCI.

A very common type of OCI is depicted in Fig. 3-23B. This optically coupled isolator is a phototransistor isolator. The phototransistor is the detector device. The use of a transistor detector also supplies the necessary gain required to interface the OCI with digital logic circuitry. The phototransistor types have certain disadvantages, the major one being bandwidth. The typical bandwidth is limited to approximately 100 kHz because the same physical structure within the phototransistor must both detect and amplify the resulting photocurrent. The large capacitance between the transistor's base and collector is the prime factor limiting the operating bandwidth of the phototransistor OCI.

By changing the detector of the OCI, we can increase the operating bandwidth. If we choose a photodiode as the detector and use a high-frequency transistor as an amplifier, we can greatly increase the available bandwidth. This type of OCI is pictured in Fig. 3-23C and is appropriately called a photodiode/transistor isolator. By separating the detector (photodiode) from the amplifier (high-frequency transistor), we reduce the feedback capacitance from about 15 pF in the phototransistor OCIs to approximately 1 pF. With a feedback capacitance of 1 pF, we can now enjoy a device with a bandwidth reaching 20 MHz.

Fig. 3-22. Typical "minidip" package with six leads can hold all the components needed to make an optically coupled isolator. (Courtesy Monsanto.)

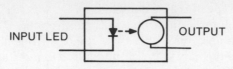

A. OPTICALLY COUPLED ISOLATOR

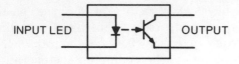

B. PHOTOTRANSISTOR ISOLATOR

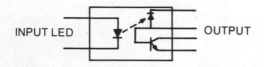

C. PHOTODIODE/TRANSISTOR ISOLATOR

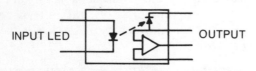

D. PHOTODIODE/IC ISOLATOR

Fig. 3-23. The optically coupled isolator has many variations.

We also have a more sophisticated type of OCI that still contains the photodiode as the detector, but also includes an integrated circuit. This IC can be a digital logic gate or an integrated operational amplifier (op-amp). A typical OCI incorporating an integrated circuit is Hewlett Packard's 5082–4360 line of OCIs, which uses a gallium arsenide phosphide LED as the input diode and a monolithic integrated detector. The detector consists of a photodiode followed by a linear amplifier that drives a Schottky-clamped output transistor. Figure 3-23D shows the internal structure. Hewlett Packard's unit incorporates an output circuit that is temperature, voltage, and current compensated to be truly compatible with standard TTL and DTL logic circuits.

Optically coupled isolators have found their way into the field of analog as well as digital circuits. For an OCI to be used in analog circuits, the basic requirement is that the output be a more-or-less linear function of the input signal. In many instances the OCI must also operate quite linearly if it is to be incorporated into a precision analog circuit. With devices other than OCIs, inverse or negative feedback may be used to control the linearity of the device. With OCIs inverse feedback cannot be directly applied, since the purpose of using an OCI is to completely isolate the input from the output.

Chapter 4
Arrays
and Displays

Many of the arrays in this chapter contain LEDs and photodetectors, either together or separate. We will first discuss photodetector devices.

PHOTODETECTOR ARRAYS

A phototransistor, for sake of simplicity, can be regarded as a photosensitive diode in parallel with the collector-base junction of a silicon NPN transistor (Fig. 4-1). As the base current increases, collector voltage V_{CE} may decrease. If V_{CE} becomes equal in magnitude to V_{BE}, the *photocurrent* source becomes a *photovoltaic* source, allowing the transistor to run into saturation. In conventional circuitry, the phototransistor is used in the indentical manner that a ordinary transistor would be, except that the base terminal of the phototransistor is usually left open. Phototransistors are designed for low leakage in order to operate this way. However, the following considerations must be observed. The *Miller effect* is the effect that capacitance C_{ob} has on time parameters; C_{ob} is multiplied by the transistor's h_{FE} (beta or DC current gain). Thermal leakage is also important with the base open in the transistor circuitry, since the device is more susceptible to thermally induced collector-base leakage; this effect can also be multiplied by the transistors h_{FE}.

The following circuits are shown using discrete components rather than arrays to allow you to see photodetectors in operation first.

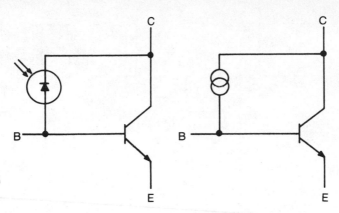

Fig. 4-1. A phototransistor can be viewed as a photodiode in parallel with the collector-base junction of a silicon transistor.

Figure 4-2 illustrates a smoke detector. Here, the light level is preset by the variable current-limiting resistor. If smoke is present between the light source (LED) and the phototransistor, the current will decrease as the light level reaching the phototransistor decreases, thus upsetting the balance of the bridge.

In Fig. 4-3 we have a basic burglar alarm circuit. Here, an encoded (modulated) beam from an LED strikes a

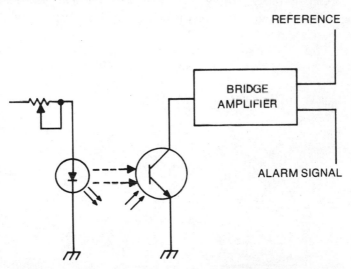

Fig. 4-2. An LED and a phototransistor can make an effective smoke detector. As the light level reaching the phototransistor drops, the bridge amplifier becomes unbalanced. In the unbalanced position, a signal is generated.

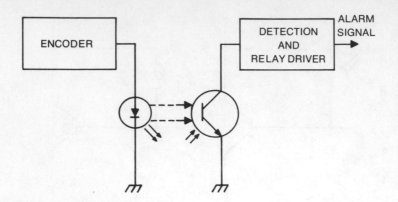

Fig. 4-3. This circuit is similiar to the smoke detector, except that the LED is now modulated. The modulated beam cannot be tampered with.

phototransistor. As long as the beam continues to strike the photodevice, the alarm is kept in the off state. But as soon as the beam is stopped (interrupted), the associated equipment will sound an alarm.

In this circuit the encoding is important. First, to keep stray ambient light or radiation from interfering with the circuit. And second, so that intruders cannot use their own light source to fool the phototransister. The phototransistor and its associated equipment is designed to recognize only the encoded beam of light.

In both the smoke detector and burglar alarm, an IR LED is the best source of irradiance. The IR radiation is not

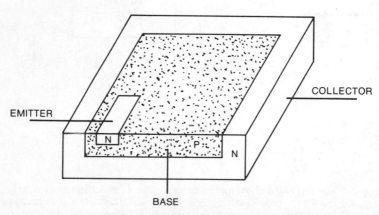

Fig. 4-4. The internal structure of an NPN phototransistor.

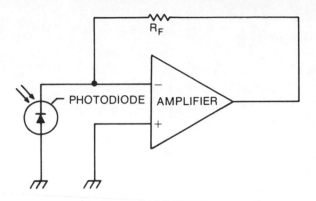

Fig. 4-5. The output of the photodiode amplifier may be viewed on an oscilloscope or a pulse counter.

perceivable by the eye, and photodevices are usually more sensitive in this region of the electromagnetic spectrum.

If the emitter is left open and the base and collector are used in the phototransistor, we can consider the device now to be a photodiode. Figure 4-4 shows the internal structure of the phototransistor device. Using the phototransistor as a photodiode, we can create circuits such as Fig. 4-5, which is a photodiode amplifier. By using a phototransistor as a photodiode, we lose sensitivity but gain response speed. This type of circuit can be used to measure light pulses with the output of the amplifier (IC amplifiers such as the 741, 709, etc.) fed into an event counter or viewed on an oscilloscope.

A simple array can be made by housing an LED and a phototransistor in the same package. Such devices are called *irradiance reflection emitter/sensor arrays*. They generally consist of a gallium arsenide infrared-emitting diode and a silicon NPN transistor. The axial radiant intensity of the IR LED and the axial response of the phototransistor are both perpendicular to the face of the device. The phototransistor therefore responds to radiation emitted from the diode only when a reflective object or surface is in the field of view of the phototransistor. Figure 4-6 shows the basic package format, while Fig. 4-7 shows the operating mode. This device finds itself being used in quite a few different areas, such as detecting the beginning and end of an object, reading marks and distance measurements, and looking for holes in objects from one side (Fig. 4-8).

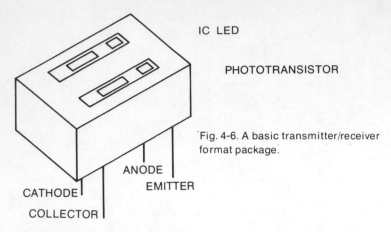

IC LED

PHOTOTRANSISTOR

Fig. 4-6. A basic transmitter/receiver format package.

ANODE
EMITTER
CATHODE
COLLECTOR

In chromochemistry a chemical reaction changes the color of a substance or solution when the reaction occurs, thus causing a change in the current through the phototransistor. Of course, the color doesn't have to change. In some reactions a precipitate may be formed, or a solution that was clear may become opaque.

We also have "pure" arrays—arrays composed of only photodetectors or photoemitters. An array that is quite interesting and unique is the photodiode array. Some of these arrays consist of 128 or more elements. Such devices are

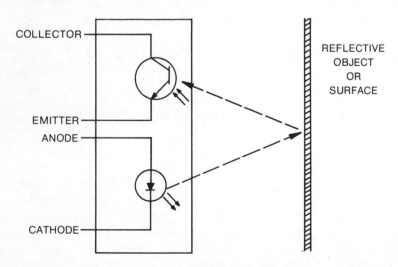

Fig. 4-7. The transmitter/receiver can be used as a source detector in an event counter.

84

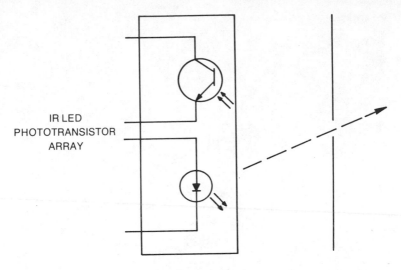

IR LED
PHOTOTRANSISTOR
ARRAY

Fig. 4-8. When the beam is not reflected, the phototransistor goes into cut-off, and the hole is detected.

useful in areas where precise scanning is required. Obviously, the greater the number of elements, the greater the resolution of the system.

These photodiode arrays can be used as the scanning element in a circuit that reads print, for example. A few different companies have done research into equipment that can literally be the eyes for a blind person. Such devices scan printed matter word by word, review their internal memories for the sound patterns, and use some sort of audio generator to sound the word. This type of apparatus could also supply a tactile response instead.

Phototransistors also come in arrays, although usually with not as many elements per array as that of the photodiode units. These arrays usually contain 20 or less elements. Most card readers employ arrays consisting of NPN planar phototransistors.

LED ARRAYS

Of course, there are also LED arrays. There are three basic types: 5-by-7 matrix, seven-segment, and straight-line arrays. The 5-by-7 matrix and the seven-segment arrays are usually called *character* displays. Figure 4-9 is a typical seven-segment display. Light-emitting diode displays are appearing everywhere. The reasons are obvious; they are

Fig. 4-9. Seven-segment LED displays. (Courtesy Monsanto.)

small in comparison with their non-solid-state counterparts. In portable equipment their low power requirement makes them extremely attractive. As we stated before, LED arrays can be of two sorts *common anode* or *common cathode*. Using the common-anode display, the decoder-driver (the circuitry that activiates the different elements of the array) must *sink* current, whereas the decoder/driver for common-cathode arrays must *source* current.

Electrically, the solid-state lamp is similiar to the solid-state diode with its inherent characteristics. Below the knee of the current-vs-voltage curve, it passes little current. Above the knee, current increases linearly with voltage. Rather than a constant voltage, a constant current is required for uniform brightness of each segment. In the normal operating mode, the radiant output increases linearly with current, and current must be limited to protect the device in question.

The basic display circuit consists of a simple resistor and power supply, in conjunction with switches that are used to actuate each segment of a digit. In practice, the LED readouts are controlled by digital circuitry instead of switches; of course, digital logic circuitry could be regarded as a complex form of solid-state switching. The digits are normally driven by decoders, which in turn are driven by logic circuits whose outputs are in either binary-coded decimal (BCD) or decimal format.

BCD is perhaps the most common form of coding. BCD code is an 8-4-2-1 type of code that employs four-digit binary combinations to represent each of the 10 digits (decimal) from 0 to 9. The binary place values depend on powers of 2, such that the left-most binary digit in BCD code has a value of 8 and the right-most digit has a value of 1. Table 4-1 gives the BCD equivalent for the decimal digits 0 to 9.

Integrated circuits are readily available to convert BCD (four-line BCD) into an appropriate seven-segment format to drive the displays. Two general techniques are used to drive seven-segment displays in which the decoding function is performed externally to the display (there are also LED displays that contain complete decoding and driving circuits). In *direct drive* or *DC mode*, which is usually used when there are four or less digits involved, the display is operated with each character illuminated at all times. A decoder/driver is therefore required for each display character.

The second technique, called *multiplexing*, is the only logical method to use to reduce the number of components in a multidigit system. In multiplexing there is only one decoder/driver circuit, and this one decoder/driver is *time-shared* among the many digits in the display. The digits are illuminated at a pulse rate fast enough that no perceptible

Table 4-1. Decimal and BCD Equivalents

DECIMAL	BCD
0	0000
1	0001
2	0010
3	0011
4	0100
5	0101
6	0110
7	0111
8	1000
9	1001

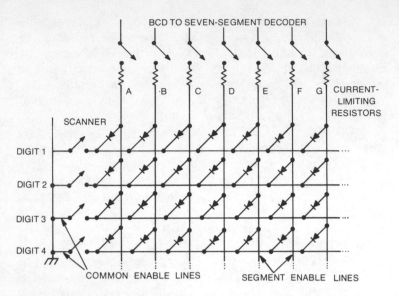

BCD TO SEVEN-SEGMENT DECODER

Fig. 4-10. A multiplexing circuit can be symbolically shown by a matrix of LEDs and enabling switches.

flicker exists. Because the human eye detects the average output, a low duty cycle with a high peak-current pulse applied to each display will provide the same subjective appearance as a continuous current would at lower but steady values. Since LEDs have exceedingly short electrical and optical rise times, they can be multiplexed with a low duty cycle and a high scanning rate. Designers usually choose a minimum scanning rate of 100 Hz.

In order to achieve a brightness level equivalent to static DC operation, the current that is pulsed to each display must be increased in magnitude proportionally to the number of displays involved in the multiplexing system. If n number of displays are to be multiplexed, approximately n times the current is required to drive a single display to the desired brightness level.

The ideal multiplex circuit as shown in Fig. 4-10 would consist of a decoder/driver that would be either a constant current source or a constant current sink. Of course, the type of decoder/driver would depend on whether the LED display had common-anode or common-cathode terminations. The display-addressing system should be a low-resistance switch. Unfortunately, this is true only in the ideal circuit.

88

A typical multiplex circuit is shown in block form in Fig. 4-11. A clock input is required to determine the multiplexing rate of the system. This clock circuit is usually an astable multivibrator, which is a symmetrical circuit containing two sections (these may be transistors or complete logic circuits), one of which controls the state of the other. If one section is on, the other section is off.

Multivibrator circuits operate in an on/off mode, so they are ideally suited for digital circuits. One of these uses is to provide timing signals (the clock function). The *astable* (free-running) multivibrator changes the state of its two sections periodically without need for input pulses, as opposed to the *monostable* multivibrator (single-shot) that supplies only one change of state per input pulse. (After a predetermined period of time, the monostable will return to its former state.) The free-running circuit is usually the choice made for the clock, since it can supply pulses to the rest of the circuit. Figure 4-12 shows a basic astable multivibrator designed with two NOR logic gates.

There are other forms of multivibrators such as the *bistable* type in which an input signal will cause it to change states, but it will not return to its former state. The monostable is stable in only one state and will always return to it.

We also need a scan counter, which will address the scan decoder and input address selector. The scan decoder selects the individual display that is to be energized, supplying that display with power, or in some cases with a ground.

The input address selector is sometimes called a multiplexer or shift register. It receives the BCD input data that is to be displayed via the decoder/driver. The decoder/driver receives the BCD inputs and decodes them to the seven-segment format (or other format, depending on the display type).

We will discuss the common-cathode display system first. In the common-cathode system, the appropriate anode (segment) enable lines are energized for the character to be displayed (Fig. 4-11). One common-cathode (digit) line is also energized to select the proper display location. The scanner then proceeds to the next display digit or character position and activates its common enable line and the appropriate segment enable lines. The current-limiting resistors are placed in the segment enable lines so that uneven current distribution will be prevented.

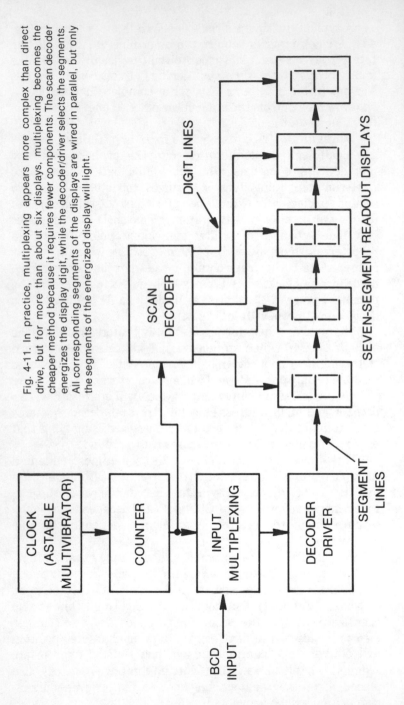

Fig. 4-11. In practice, multiplexing appears more complex than direct drive, but for more than about six displays, multiplexing becomes the cheaper method because it requires fewer components. The scan decoder energizes the display digit, while the decoder/driver selects the segments. All corresponding segments of the displays are wired in parallel, but only the segments of the energized display will light.

CLOCK (ASTABLE MULTIVIBRATOR)

COUNTER

INPUT MULTIPLEXING

BCD INPUT

DECODER DRIVER

SCAN DECODER

DIGIT LINES

SEGMENT LINES

SEVEN-SEGMENT READOUT DISPLAYS

Transistors are normally used as the switches in a decoder/driver. These transistors may be discrete or in the form of an IC. The activation of a particular digit segment requires that the corresponding digit driver transistor and a segment driver transistor be turned on at the same time. The energizing of an additional segment of the same digit merely requires that another segment driver transistor be turned on. A different digit or display is energized by turning on its corresponding digit driver transistor.

It should be pointed out that each display must have its own digit drive transistor, whereas the segments are wired in parallel to each display and thus share the same segment driver transistor. It is here that multiplexing saves components by sharing transistors and saving leads. Each similar segment of the different display units share the same segment enable lines. For example, a display having six seven-segment readouts would require $6 \times 7 = 42$ driver transistors in a direct-drive system, but only $6 + 7 = 13$ drivers in a multiplex system.

It should be noted at this point that all seven-segment displays use the same labeling for their segments (see Fig. 4-13).

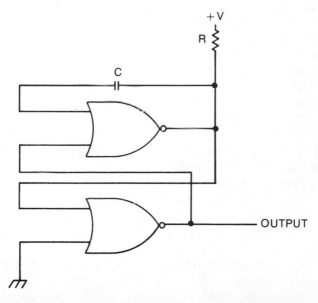

Fig. 4-12. A basic astable multivibrator. The resistor and capacitor control the pulse frequency.

91

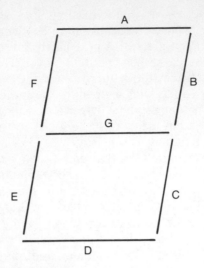

Fig. 4-13. The seven-segment readout has common labeling, without regard to manufacturer.

Whether the multiplexing system uses common-anode or common-cathode displays, the same number of components is required. In Fig. 4-14, we have a typical common-anode display system (at this point, we are not going to discuss how this circuit operates or what it does outside of the discussion on display enabling). Transistors Q1 to Q7 are the cathode-segment enable drivers, while transistors Q8 to Q15 are the common-anode display enable drivers. Figure 4-15 shows basically the same circuitry, except that it is a common-cathode system.

ALPHANUMERIC MATRIX SCANNING

Figure 4-16 is a sample of the typical alphanumeric display in use. The alphanumeric display consists of an array of 5-by-7 light-emitting diodes. The array is X-Y (row-column) addressable, which allows easy driving, decoding, and addressing. The 5-by-7 matrix provides the least number of electrical connection pins required for the number of LEDs addressed.

X-Y addressing is also better since it can be used with a read-only-memory (ROM) character generator. Typically, one ROM can be used with 25 or more 5-by-7 matrixes if X-Y addressing is used. To generate alphanumeric characters using the 5-by-7 matrix, a method called *strobing* or *scanning*

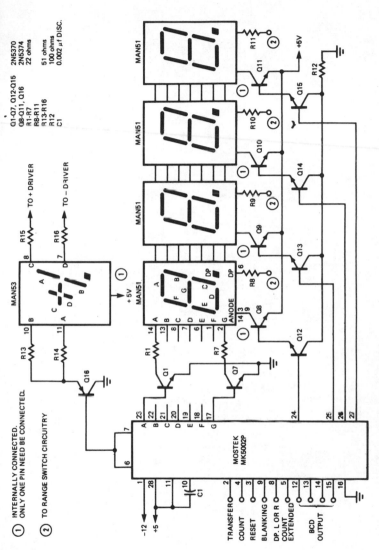

Fig. 4-14. Typical common-anode display system. (Courtesy Monsanto.)

93

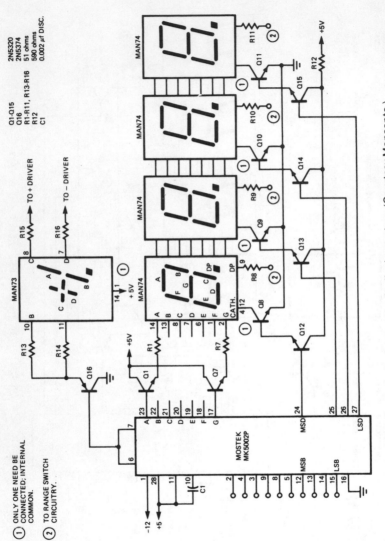

Fig. 4-15. Typical common-cathode display system. (Courtesy Monsanto.)

94

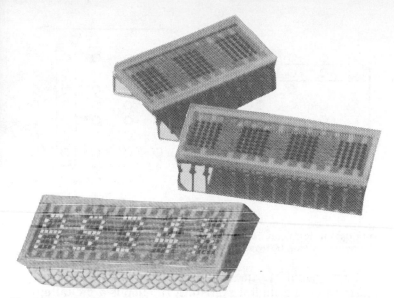

Fig. 4-16. An alphanumeric matrix commonly consists of five columns and seven rows of light-emitting elements. Because of the large number (35) of elements in the matrix, it is possible to form just about any number, letter, or symbol desired. (Courtesy Hewlett-Packard.)

is used. Information is addressed to the display by selecting one row (or one column) of diodes at a time and energizing the appropriate light-emitting diodes in that row. Then the process continues with the next row.

This method is basically a time-sharing technique between rows (or columns) of the display. After all rows have been selected in the proper order, the procedure is repeated. If the scanning frequency is carried out at around 100 times per second, a flicker-free character will be formed. When the information is strobed from row to row, top to bottom, the display mode is called *vertical* strobing. If the information is scanned column to column, left to right, the mode is called *horizontal* strobing. Figure 4-17 shows these two scanning modes.

Scan Circuitry

The associated circuitry needed to perform the high-speed sequential switching between rows or columns of light-emitting diodes in scanning can be classified into four major digital parts: storage buffers, clock timing, read-only memory, and drivers.

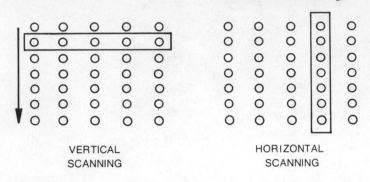

VERTICAL
SCANNING

HORIZONTAL
SCANNING

Fig. 4-17. The 5-by-7 matrix can be scanned by either vertical or horizontal methods. Vertical scanning is generally from top to bottom, while horizontal scanning is usually from left to right.

Storage buffers are flip-flops that store input or output information in a digital system. A flip-flop is a digital circuit having two stable states (bistable), and usually remains in one of these states until a pulse (or clock pulse) is applied to the flip-flop to make it change states.

Clock-timing circuitry is required to time and provide starting pulses to all the different sections of the complete circuitry. Usually, a sequential pulse generator is used for this operation.

A read-only memory (ROM) is the character generator that accepts a binary-coded input and provides the sequential 5-by-7 LED array information.

Row drivers provide the proper current drive to the LEDs making up the 5-by-7 dot array.

All of these sections could be fabricated from discrete components, but for sake of simplicity and cost, integrated circuits are generally used in this application.

Horizontal Scanning

A horizontal scanning circuit, shown in Fig. 4-18 in block form, operates as follows. Coded 6-bit (*binary digit*) alphanumeric information from the keyboard is sequentially entered and stored in three 6-bit input storage buffers. The input information code could be any code, but in this example ASCII is used. ASCII stands for American Standard Code for Information Interface and is a standard binary code used to represent common symbols and alphanumeric characters.

Information is entered 6 bits at a time in parallel to the appropriate input storage buffer, which holds one character. An array select line steers the information to the proper storage buffer.

The next function is to control the activation and enabling circuitry of the ROM and input buffers. This is done by the timing and clock circuitry. With the information stored in the input buffers, the clock-timing circuitry enables the ROM and the first input storage buffer. The buffer's stored 6-bit code information is then read into the ROM. Of course, at this time all other storage buffers are disabled. The read-only memory decodes the 6-bit input information into 7-line output. The row drivers convert the voltage output of the ROM into a current source. At the same time the output signal appears at the appropriate rows, the clock-timing circuitry connects the first column of the first LED character display to complete the circuit path and enable the appropriate diodes to light. The ROM is next triggered by a timing pulse to present the second column of character information at its 7-line output. The same procedure is then carried as before to illuminate the remaining columns, three, four, and five.

After tracing out the first character, the clock-timing circuitry enables the second input storage buffer and this information is presented to the ROM, which in turn sequentially presents the information to the second light-emitting diode display. This method continues to all the remaining character displays. When this cycle is repeated at a rate of 100 times per second or faster, a flicker-free group of characters are visible.

In Fig. 4-18 we have 15 vertical columns, making a duty cycle for the display of about 6.6%. The peak current supplied to the light-emitting diodes must then be about 15 times their average current. This high peak current usually makes necessary the use of discrete transistors as drivers because the peak current demand may be as high as 75 mA for all the LEDs in a given row or column.

With horizontal scanning techniques, the number of vertical columns that can be energized in one field of scan is limited by the peak current that any one LED can stand. The peak current limit of any one LED used in the 5-by-7 matrix is about 100 mA, and the LEDs used require approximately 5 mA for 100 foot-lamberts. Thus, about 20 columns can be run at maximum with the horizontal strobing technique.

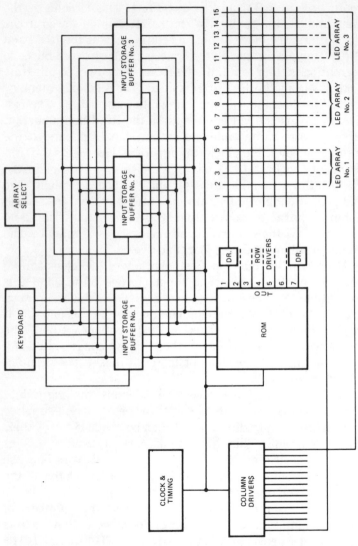

Fig. 4-18. Block diagram of horizontal scanning circuit using three readouts. (Courtesy Hewlett-Packard.)

Vertical Scanning

The technique of vertical scanning or strobing is employed for applications requiring more than four characters. This mode of operation is similiar to that of horizontal scanning, except that the scanning field moves vertically along the seven horizontal rows. This method enjoys the advantages of being able to employ more arrays in the circuitry without affecting the display's *on* duty cycle. This method will be described in detail since it is the preferred mode.

The vertical scanning system can be divided into three areas in reference to circuitry. These areas are the clock-timing circuits, the storage buffers and read-only memory, and the current-limiting and driver stages. Figure 4-19 shows the basic block diagram of the vertical (row) strobing circuitry.

Information in the form of ASCII code is entered and stored in a series of input storage buffers. The circuit as described here utilizes a keyboard that provides both an ASCII code as well as an advance timing pulse. Only one input storage buffer is enabled at a time, similar to the circuitry of the horizontal (column) scanning mode. The advance pulse from the keyboard permits the clock-timing circuitry to enable the next input storage buffer. The timing circuitry also controls the entry of information from the input buffer to the ROM. The resulting ROM-generated character is then steered to the correct output storage buffer by the clock-timing circuitry.

In the scanning circuit shown, a binary counter and decoder provide the gating pulses for the storage buffers. If the number of arrays (5-by-7 matrixes) in the display is N_A, the binary counter's reset line is connected for counting up to N_A. As the binary counter cycles through its counting sequence, timing pulses are delivered simultaneously to the input and output buffers to select the character to be displayed. The output of the selected input buffer is enabled, permitting the character to be decoded in the ROM, and the information is stored in the input portion of the selected output buffer. The outputs of the output buffer then feed the column drivers.

The output storage buffer's load time (typically 50 nsec), the read-only memory's access time (typically 1 μsec), the minimum field rate, and the line duty cycle, all dictate how many arrays can be matched with a single ROM. With a field rate of 140 Hz and a 90% row duty cycle, up to 100 arrays could be serviced by one ROM. The 140 Hz field rate is well beyond the point where flicker could occur to the human eye.

The input section of the array circuitry is probably the most flexible in nature. The incoming information may be either serial or parallel ASCII code as it is fed to each input buffer, or it may be of many other forms. Nevertheless, the basic function of the input storage buffers is to store the 6- or 7-bit ASCII code.

Returning to Fig. 4-19 for a moment, note that all input storage buffers have *parallel* outputs to the read-only memory. The read-only memory is an electronic circuit whose function is to pair an input code to its corresponding output, so the entire input is required in parallel, not serial. The ROM devices used in the illustrations involving the 5-by-7 matrixes of LEDs, provide 35 points of character-font data for displaying any one of the 64 different alphanumeric characters and symbols in the ASCII code. Thus, a total of 2240 bits of information is held in the ROM.

Whenever a timing pulse from the clock-timing circuitry is applied to the input storage buffers, the buffers' ASCII information is presented to the input of the ROM device. The ROM could be used to decode all 35 bits of an ASCII coded character and store them in a read/write memory, but this would be relatively expensive. So a modified and less expensive approach is shown in Fig. 4-19 to decode 5 bits at a time (the bits for one column). The sequence used is similiar to that of the horizontal mode, though, and there are as many input and output storage buffers as there are characters to be displayed.

After the output storage buffers are loaded with the information for column drive, the appropriate horizontal row is activated to complete the electrical circuit path. For example, in row 1 the clock-timing circuitry energizes the row-1 driver. This procedure allows any light-emitting diode on row 1 to light if its vertical column driver is turned on. If we ignore the relatively short loading time, the display cycle for seven line characters is 1/7, or approximately 14% of the total *on* time. Field rate is defined as the rate of refreshing the whole display, so if the field rate is 125 Hz, the *on* time for each row is 1150 microseconds. The LEDs are only on for 1/7 of time

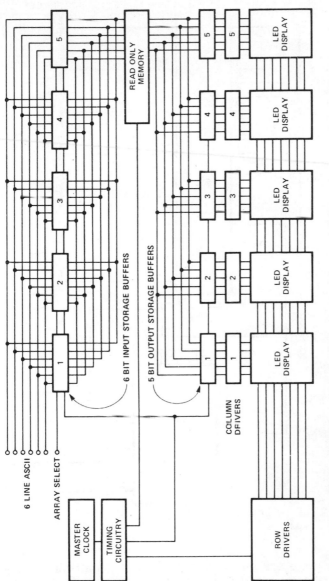

Fig. 4-19. Vertical scanning is preferred for more than four matrix displays. This block diagram illustrates a vertical scanning system for driving five readouts. The input is ASCII code, which provides a full range of display characters and symbols. (Courtesy Hewlett-Packard.)

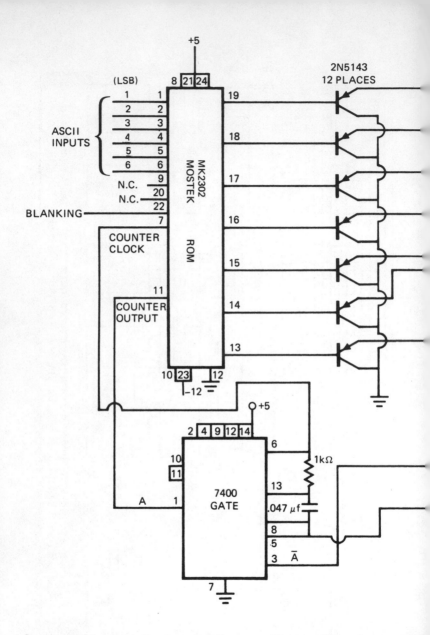

because there are 7 rows and they are lit on a time-sharing basis, and they must therefore be driven at high peak currents. For the human eye to average the light output of the LEDs used in the 5-by-7 matrixes, the diodes must be driven with a current that is seven times the average current. Assuming

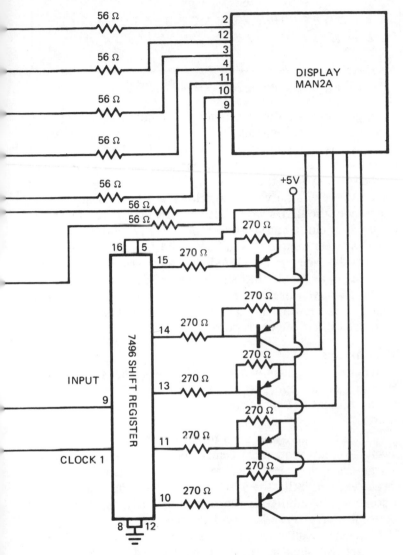

Fig. 4-20. A complete scanning decoder system. (Courtesy Monsanto.)

that the LEDs require 5 mA average current for a light output of 100 foot-lamberts, the column drivers must handle 35 mA. Here again, discrete transistors may be used, but because of the lower peak current, *power gates*—high power-handling digital logic gates—may be used.

```
0  1  2  3  4  5  6  7  8  9
A B C D E F G H I J K L M N O P Q R S T U V W X Y Z
@ - $ & ! # * , . + — / ; = ? : " % ' \ [ ] > < ( ) ^
```

Fig. 4-21. ASCII characters for six-line input code.

Light-emitting diode efficiency increases with operating current, so the efficiency of the display may be increased through this strobing process. By changing the duty cycle of the row drivers, it is also easy to change or adjust the intensity of the display's output. That is, if the *on* time for each horizontal row is halved (the field rate is kept constant), the intensity of the LEDs would also be halved. Figure 4-20 shows a typical circuit using a 5-by-7 matrix array. In this case only one character display is used. The LED array used is a 35-diode diffused planar GaAsP alphanumeric display with a decimal point. Figure 4-21 shows the 64 ASCII characters that can be displayed in the shortened 6-line code. (The full 7-line code includes lower-case letters and other less used symbols, making a total of 128 characters.)

Other Arrays

There are character-displaying arrays other than the two main ones we have just discussed (5-by-7 matrix and the seven-segment). There are also 4-by-7 arrays and linear arrays.

The 4-by-7 array is used often as a replacement for the seven-segment readout. Because of its dot patterns, more characters can be formed with it than with the seven-segment. Still, the 5-by-7 array is most flexible because it possesses the ability to reproduce the maximum number of different characters. Figure 4-22 shows some typical 4-by-7 LED arrays used as numeric and hexadecimal indicators. Some arrays, such as the Hewlett-Packard 5082-7300 series, contain on-board logic circuitry, including both a decoder/driver and memory functions. The internal circuitry of such displays makes an exceptionally small layout possible, whether they are used for readouts in equipment, calculators, or the like. Since the readout contains its own integral logic circuitry, the display is easy to incorporate into different

104

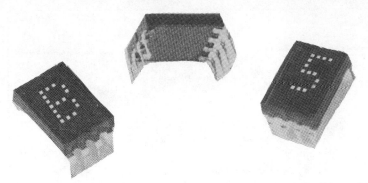

Fig. 4-22. Arrays with 4-by-7 dot patterns are not quite as flexible as the 5-by-7 arrays, but they can still display a great number of characters. Many versions do not contain a full 28 dots, but are made specifically to display the hexadecimal code that includes the numbers 0 through 9 and the letters A through F. (Courtesy Hewlett-Packard.)

display circuitries. Of course, the techniques used are not actually much different than that we have already discussed, except that less external circuitry is required in view of the display's internal components.

Linear arrays are useful items found in punched-card readers, detecting equipment, specially designed displays, and many other areas. These linear arrays may contain 50 or more discrete LEDs.

Chapter 5
New Displays and Photosensitive Devices

There are many new display devices being designed in the laboratories these days. Some are even now making their appearance outside the lab as prototypes that may some day become commonplace. Since the cathode-ray tube still dominates the field as both a display device and a photosensitive camera, it is a good idea to look at the cathode-ray tube first, since in many respects the operation of newer displays function in a very similar manner.

THE CATHODE-RAY TUBE

The cathode-ray tube (CRT) has a phosphor coating at one end and an electron gun at the other (see Figs. 5-1 and 5-2). Whether the CRT is used in an oscilloscope or in a television, black-and-white or color, or in a radar readout display, the fundamentals of CRT operation are the same.

The bulb or tube that we call the CRT contains an electron source of high potential—the accelerating voltages often exceed 40 kV. The source of clectrons is produced by the *cathode* in the tube. The electrons are "boiled" off the cathode and attracted towards the high-voltage *anode*. Before reaching the anode, a control grid and focusing anode are placed in the electron beam's path to shape the beam of emitted electrons. The electrons are accelerated as they pass through the anodes and are then directed towards their position on the fluorescent

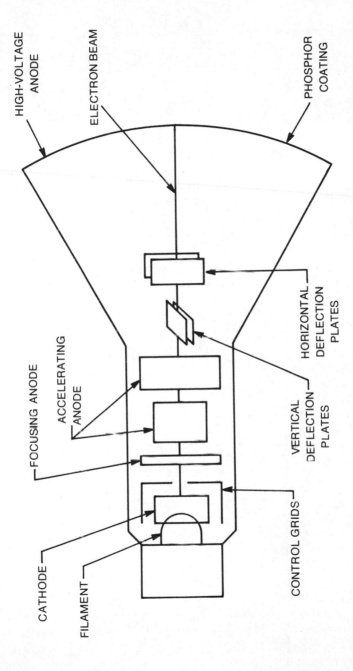

HIGH-VOLTAGE ANODE

ELECTRON BEAM

PHOSPHOR COATING

FOCUSING ANODE

ACCELERATING ANODE

HORIZONTAL DEFLECTION PLATES

VERTICAL DEFLECTION PLATES

CATHODE

FILAMENT

CONTROL GRIDS

Fig. 5-1. The electrostatic-deflection CRT uses electrostatic fields instead of magnetic fields for beam deflection.

107

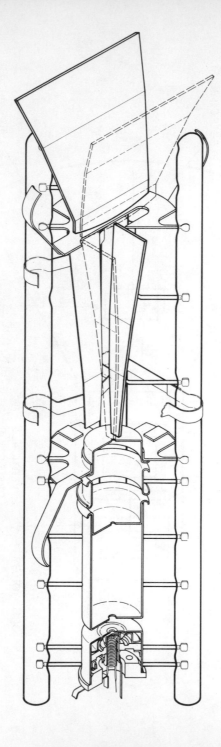

Fig. 5-2. A typical CRT electron gun. (Courtesy Tektronix.)

screen by deflection plates. There are two sets of these deflection plates (typical CRTs use either electrostatic deflection plates or magnetic deflection coils). These deflection plates control horizontal and vertical displacement of the electron beam. Once the beam strikes the phosphor coating of the screen, photons are emitted, lighting the area where the beam strikes. Depending on the phosphor used, we can obtain white or different color images.

Special circuitry is required to dictate where the beam strikes the coating of the CRT at any given point in time. The cathode-ray tube also requires a high potential voltage to operate, thus necessitating enormous power supplies. More than one manufacturer, especially those concerned with the TV industry, are researching different methods and techniques that may some day cause the CRT to become obsolete.

NEW DISPLAYS

For many years now, experimental "flatpanel" TVs have been shown around the world. Unfortunately, until recently these ultra-thin displays have been monochromatic. Rapid advances in microcircuits and new display devices seem to be finally turning the tables toward the day where the CRT will not preside over other display units. These new displays circulate around the following technologies:

- electroluminescence
- liquid crystals
- ferroelectric ceramics
- gas discharge

Up to now the main problems with these competing fields have been the life time of the display elements, the brightness level of the display, contrast ratios, and probably the most difficult area, that of actually fabricating the display.

These different approaches use different systems of supplying the desired information to the display elements. The circuits are different and the power levels change from one type to the next. For example, interconnecting the circuitry of a TV set to the display unit usually requires tremendous numbers of connectors. By using *thin-film* integrated circuit technology, combined with electroluminescent (EL) elements, the required number of interconnectors is drastically reduced.

ICs are now being fabricated that are large enough in size to generate a picture with images on their special surfaces that can readily be seen. These display units will without doubt make their appearance in the form of alphanumeric, radar, and computer information displays before they are ready to be used and manufactured on the domestic scale.

The ability to do away with the CRT—the single biggest piece of hardware in most information delivering systems, including televisions—would enable engineers to create many unique devices. The first device that pops into mind is the *wide-screen* TV, with the thickness of the display measured in fractions of an inch rather than the bulky CRTs that are often over 15 inches deep. Such devices would cause numerous innovations in the oscilloscope industry alone. Many disadvantages inherent with CRTs would finally be laid to rest. Such disadvantages as conversion and degaussing in color CRTs would not occur in solid-state or solid-state/gas-discharge units. Focusing of coils, positioning of deflection coils, and the analog nature of the CRT are limiting factors in regard to compactness and accuracy of the display.

To this date a commercially available display other than the CRT is not available (discounting small LED matrixes and the like), but research is being carried out by more than one large electronics concern. To briefly summarize what strides have been made, we will look at what the industry has produced to date.

A neon discharge system such as shown in Fig. 5-3 operates as such by *priming* the neon gas in each "cell" of the display cathodes until ionized, then using common anodes to sustain the discharge. A 40:1 contrast ratio with a brightness level of 8-foot-lamberts is achieved.

Other display methods include using electroluminescent (EL) panels. Such displays would use approximately 80% less power and would last perhaps three times longer than the CRT type of display. Where in the analog CRT an electron beam is swept across the phosphor face of the tube, the EL display uses an X-Y scanning technique similar to the X-Y matrixes discussed earlier. By addressing different points on the EL display and using vertical strobing methods, each horizontal line is activated in sequence. An addressable X-Y matrix electroluminescent panel of this nature would be scarcely thicker than 5 millimeters. Of course, with every development,

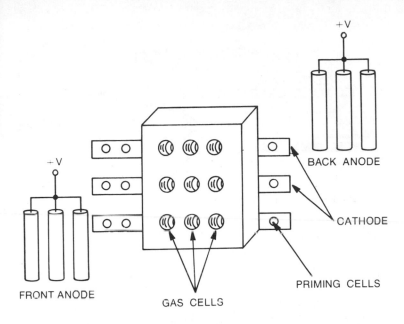

Fig. 5-3. Gas-discharge display requires both front and rear anode.

new problems do arise—there has to be a scan-line connection for every row, and an enable-line connection for every column, thus producing a display panel with hundreds of wires.

Another firm has produced a luminescent panel with over 10,000 light-producing elements. Beneath each element lies transistor circuitry, a compactness that was brought about by thin-film technology. No doubt, in the near future, complete shift-register circuits will be incorporated within the thin-film circuitry of the display, eliminating the present necessity of the hundreds of wires. Even the complete display drive and input circuitry may be placed within the structure of the display itself. A computer readout could be 5 to 10 millimeters thick with as large a surface area as desired. An enormous amount of space is saved if the scanning circuitry and the complete circuitry of the instrument is incorporated into the thin-film behind the luminescent elements.

Not only are EL panels being coupled with thin-film transistors, but also with liquid-crystal (LC) displays. This type of display is reflective in nature, as opposed to elements that provide direct illumination. Using liquid crystals for elements, the operation of the display is a little different.

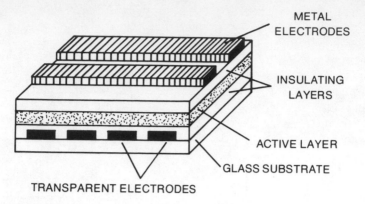

Fig. 5-4. Thin-film electroluminescent displays may provide the thin television screens of the future.

Transistors at the site of each LC element control the amount of light passing through the nematic liquid and reflecting from the polished electrodes. LC displays, unlike light-producing displays, do not wash out under strong ambient light conditions. Actually, their contrast ratios increase under more intense illumination. Nevertheless, the other types of flat displays have a head start on the LC and EL panels, if for no other reason than that less research has been done on them. Figure 5-4 shows the structure of a rather simple thin-film EL display.

Much of the research to date has been with gas-filled (neon) cells. The orange glow of the neon is not especially

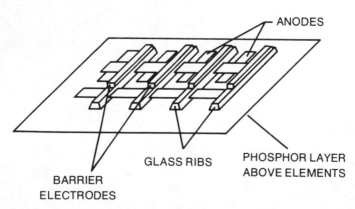

Fig. 5-5. Gas-discharge display. Another contender for the future television or oscilloscope screen.

bright (8 foot-lamberts), nor is it specifically attractive to TV viewers. But here again, methods are being worked out and tested. With the use of phosphors, the ultraviolet emission of the glowing ionized neon causes the phosphor coatings of the cells to glow white. With appropriate mixing of different types of phosphors, the triad of colors, red, green, and blue can be generated, thus creating colored images.

Another entry into the gas discharge field looks like Fig. 5-5. Bars are used instead of cells for the gas discharge, and a triad of phosphors is used to create the necessary three colors. A panel of this construction is about ¼-inch in thickness.

In the future, LED, EL, and LC displays will probably win against the others since they are solid-state devices and therefore more compatible with IC technology.

Figure 5-6 illustrates the internal construction of a typical LC valve. Even though it is rather compact, it can achieve an interesting effect. If a weak source of light images are projected onto the writing side of the LC valve, the photoconductive layer is activated and enables the LC layer (nematic liquid crystal) on the other side of the light barrier to pass light. A panel made up of these valves, with a light source appropriately arranged on the projection side of the valve, can project an image.

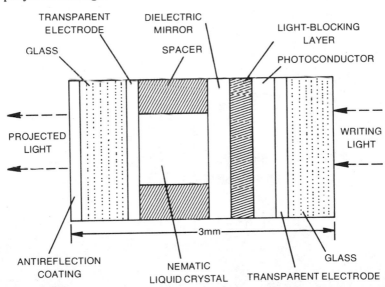

Fig. 5-6. A light valve is able to electrically control the transmission of light passing through the cell.

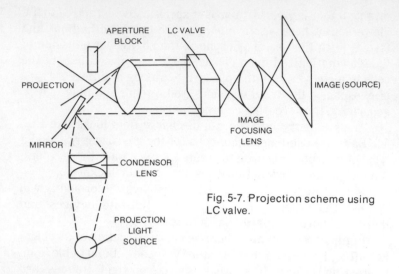

APERTURE BLOCK
LC VALVE
PROJECTION
IMAGE (SOURCE)
IMAGE FOCUSING LENS
MIRROR
CONDENSOR LENS
Fig. 5-7. Projection scheme using LC valve.
PROJECTION LIGHT SOURCE

Figure 5-7 is a possible method of using the LC valve as the controlling agent in a projection circuit. Even a color valve is possible (Fig. 5-8) by stacking three LC valves. Color transmission is controlled by selectively applying voltage to the valve designated to each color.

Another possible display is made from lanthanum-modified lead zirconate titanate (PLZT), a ferroelectric ceramic. By applying a voltage potential across

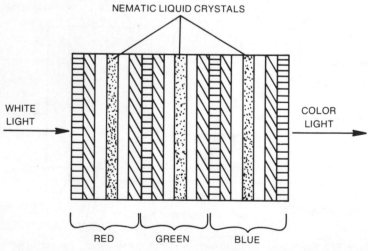

NEMATIC LIQUID CRYSTALS

WHITE LIGHT

COLOR LIGHT

RED   GREEN   BLUE

Fig. 5-8. Three-color LC valve for projecting color images.

the PLZT crystal, an image falling on the photoconductive layer reorients the PLZT's microscopic domains (Fig. 5-9). The image is then stored for projection or direct viewing. The darker images in the PLZT ceramic are caused by more domains being oriented, causing more light scattering. For display operation, a network of electrodes is placed behind the PLZT display, causing different intensities as domains are orientated by the control voltage. In this application the photoconductive layer is not required. (A display with LC valves can also be made by removing the photoconductive layers.) Either transmission or reflective modes can be used. LC devices might be reflective, while the PLZT might use an internal light source.

I have seen an interesting display using light-emitting diodes arranged in groups of three (blue, green, red). The biggest problem with this type of display (other than the current demand) is that the color blue is extremely difficult to produce in an LED lamp. The principle of operation is similar to that discussed in the chapter on 5-by-7 matrixes, except that the LEDs must also be scanned for color as well. For example, a display consisting of an array of dots, 500 by 700, can be viewed as 10,000 5-by-7 matrixes and scanned accordingly.

LED displays that use the color red only, usually have a red Plexiglas material placed in front of the display to enhance the contrast ratio of the display. Plexiglas materials such as 2423 are generally used. To further enhance the contrast, a Polaroid filter such as HRCP-red may be used. Louver-type filters may also be employed, though they reduce the viewing

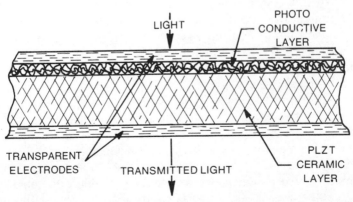

Fig. 5-9. PLZT display device.

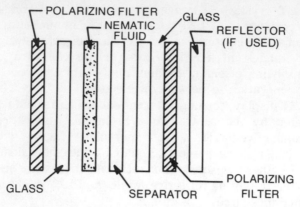

Fig. 5-10. The liquid-crystal display is fabricated with several layers of materials with only one being the nematic liquid or liquid crystal.

angle to some degree, but will significantly reduce the amount of wash-out caused by extraneous ambient light. Still another approach is the use of antiglare coatings such as are available from Panelgraphic Corp. These special coatings tend to reduce front-panel reflections, thus making it possible to view the display in strong ambient light.

LIGHT CRYSTAL DISPLAYS

Liquid crystals have become so important during the last few years that they deserve a more detailed description of their operation. The liquid crystal display (LCD) is completely different from the solid-state lamp display in one very important aspect—the LED display *generates* light, while the LC display *controls* light. To be more specific, the LED segment of the display must be continuously activated for that segment to emit light energy; the LC segment is activated or "switched" to either block or permit the passage of light, a process that consumes energy during the switching operation but not on a continuous basis.

There are two basic types of liquid crystal displays, and there are two basic ways in which light is controlled in the LC displays. In the *reflective* mode, light is introduced from the front of the display, travels through the display, reflects off a mirrored surface, and exits via the front of the display. In the *transmissive* mode, a non-ambient light source is generally placed behind the LCD and is controlled as it passes through the display. The two types of LCDs are the *dynamic scattering*

LCD, and the *field-effect* LCD. We will discuss first the field-effect LCD as it is generally favored by designers since it draws approximately 20% of the current requirement of the dynamic-scattering type, which requires about one nanoampere of current (LEDs and other displays draw currents ranging from a few milliamperes to several amperes).

The field-effect LCD consists of two pieces of glass separated by a special "crystal" liquid, called a *nematic fluid*. One of the glass sheets is coated with a very thin, transparent layer of metal, while the other piece of glass is coated with a metallization pattern of addressable, electrically isolated islands (Fig. 5-10). Polarizing filters are placed in front of and behind the glass plates. When the segments are not activated, the molecules of the nematic fluid arrange themselves parallel to the plane of the glass plates. When a voltage field is applied to the nematic fluid, the molecules rotate 90 degrees in reference to the glass plates. By this phase-shifting process, black letters (characters) on a white background are available. Figure 5-11 shows a field-effect LCD with white segments when energized, while Fig. 5-12 shows a watch utilizing black characters when activated. Changing the background color in reference to the color of the segments is controlled by rotating one of the polarizing filters 90° in relation with the other filter.

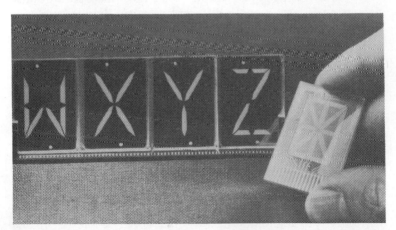

Fig. 5-11. Alphanumeric liquid-crystal displays contain 14 segments to produce all numbers, letters, and many special symbols. A polarizing filter covers the front of the four displays at left, allowing only the activated segments to be seen. (Courtesy Hamlin Inc.)

Fig. 5-12. A solid-state watch with a liquid-crystal display. (Courtesy Hamlin, Inc.)

Dynamic-scattering LCDs do not incorporate any polarizing filters, since a different nematic fluid is used that turns milky-white in color when a voltage is applied to the segments.

Both the dynamic-scattering and the field-effect LCDs can use reflective or transmissive modes of display. In either case, only an AC voltage should ever be applied to the LCD. If any DC offset voltage is present, this can reduce the life expectancy of the display drastically—if not immediately destroy the liquid crystal display. The applied AC field need not be sinusiodal and rarely is. Generally, a square-wave signal is used to activate the display, with a voltage potential comparable with that used for the ICs driving the LCD.

The backplane of the LCD receives the electric potential field, and the segments are switched either to the backplane (the glass plate completely coated with metal) or to the output of an inverter, which supplies a 180° phase-shifted signal. By switching the segments to the backplane, the segment is shorted out; switching the segment to the output of an inverter causes the segment to turn on.

Switching is extremely important in LCDs as their impedances are in the vicinity of a gigaohm (10^9 ohms), with a capacitance of about 200 pF. Typically, most mechanical switches are prone to leak current to the LCD, thus turning on segments spuriously. An electronic logic gate such as the exclusive-OR (XOR) is generally used for the switching functions in circuitry involving liquid crystal displays because the XOR gate provides an in-phase signal to the segments when the gate is low or off, and a out-of-phase (180°) signal to the segments when the gate is high or on. CMOS ICs are also used because they represent a pure resistance to the LCD when in the low state, while DTL or TTL ICs include diodes that can introduce DC voltage to the display when they are in the low state. CMOS also switches between *supply voltage* to *ground*, where TTL, for example, switches from nominal *5V* to about *0.6V* (the 0.6V level can cause DC offset).

The duty cycle must always be 50%. If any other duty cycle is chosen, DC offset will occur. Usually, the applied frequency ranges from 32 Hz to a maximum of 50 Hz, with the 32 Hz considered optimum. Figure 5-13 shows a mechanical

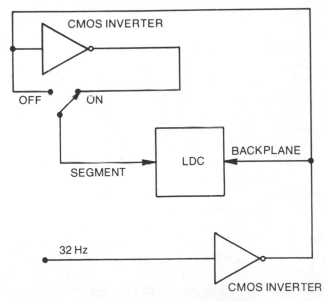

Fig. 5-13. A typical LCD driving circuit.

119

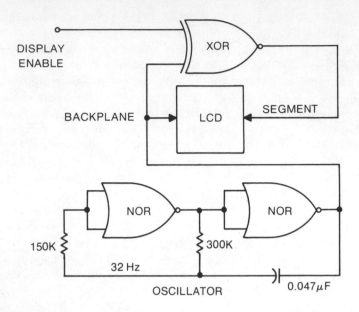

DISPLAY
ENABLE

XOR

BACKPLANE

LCD

SEGMENT

NOR

NOR

150K

32 Hz

300K

OSCILLATOR

0.047μF

Fig. 5-14. An actual LCD driving circuit requires at least an oscillator and an electronic switch.

type of switching for an LCD, while Fig. 5-14 shows a method with XOR gates. Also in Fig. 5-14 is a basic oscillator using NOR gates for the generation of the required 32 Hz signal.

LCDs can be used where the speed of response is not expected to be high, such as in a digital watch. Where high-speed response is required, such as in digital voltmeters, the light-emitting diode display is preferable. And temperature is also a major consideration with LCDs, since at about 0°C (32°F) the response speed of the LCD drops to approximately one second, while at temperatures over 50°C (122°F) the nematic fluid is destroyed.

In a dark environment, where very little ambient light is present, an internal light is required with LCDs. An LED, of course, produces its own light. The addition of a light source to the LCD defeats the low-power advantage that it possesses over LEDs. But one American manufacturer of watches got around this obstacle by sealing a phosphor-tritium compound in a glass ampule mounted behind the LCD readout. During periods of low ambient light, the glow from the phosphor compound permitted the readout to be seen, in much the same manner as with conventional watches having luminous phosphor painted on the hour and minute hands. The advantage of using phosphor in this manner is that no power supply is required to make the phosphor glow, and therefore the life of the watch battery is unaffected.

In general, field-effect LCDs are more readable in bright ambient lighting than dynamic-scattering LCDs. In fact, field-effect LCDs are even more readable than LEDs in which the display tends to wash out under the competing lights, whereas the LCD maintains its readability because it simply reflects back more light. The power consumption of the LCD remains unchanged under all lighting conditions, staying in the nanoampere range, while the LED must increase drive current to remain readable under bright lights.

Another advantage that LCDs have over LEDs is that of size. For example, the large alphanumeric display in Fig. 5-15 still draws only a few nanoamperes. An LED display of comparable size would be much more expensive and would require many hundreds of milliamperes. It is true that such a large LED display would be quite readable, but such displays would normally be found in groups, further increasing the cost

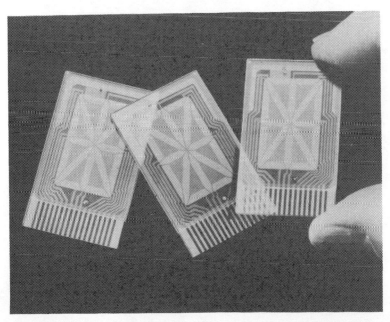

Fig. 5-15. Liquid crystal displays come in fairly large sizes. (Courtesy Hamlin, Inc.)

and current requirements, especially if multiplexing is required.

IMAGE SENSORS

The new solid-state image sensors are specially fabricated and designed integrated circuits. A single monolithic chip of silicon may contain thousands of photosensitive devices. These special ICs are mounted in normal IC packages, except that the top is made of transparent material.

The photosensitive elements are scanned as an image strikes the IC. This produces an electronic analog video signal. These ICs are usually either *linear* or *area* arrays—that is, the photosensitive elements are either in a straight line (linear) or in a two-dimensional array (area).

The linear array can also be used to create two-dimensional pictures, but it must be scanned line by line as the image moves across the sensor. In other words, only one line of information can be displayed at a time because the sensor is only capable of detecting one line of information at a time.

Whether the sensor is linear or area, the greater the number of sensors employed, the greater the resolution of the system. The big advantage the area array has over the linear is that the necessity of mechanically scanning the image from top to bottom is eliminated.

Solid-state image sensors are proving themselves, especially in the field of optical devices designed to aid the blind. The output of circuits employing these image sensors can provide tactile feedback, or even the spoken word. The image sensor itself can be made by different methods. The most common forms are the charge-coupled device (CCD) and the MOS scanned-photodiode array. In both cases, the inherent light-sensitive properties of silicon are exploited.

Silicon in the presence of light undergoes a process called *photogeneration*—when light interacts with the silicon material, current carriers are generated. Both holes and electrons are produced in this process. With the production of these current carriers, the resistance of the silicon decreases. Typically, for each photon that impinges upon the silicon, one electron-hole pair is created. Unfortunately, though, silicon is not uniformly sensitive to all wavelengths of radiant energy, but becomes more sensitive as we progress from red light and down into the infrared region of the electromagnetic spectrum (Fig. 5-16).

CHARGE-COUPLED DEVICES

CCDs have an advantage over the MOS scanned-photodiode array in that their packing density can be significantly increased. The basic photosensitive device in the CCD is a MOS type capacitor, in which the important feature is that the charge can be carried or transferred sideways across the image sensor. When radiant energy strikes a MOS capacitor element in the array, a charge is generated through photogeneration. The greater the intensity of the radiant energy, the greater the charge generated. Video information is then read out by rapidly transferring the charge from the illuminated MOS capacitors to adjacent capacitors until the charge reaches the measuring electrodes.

The largest commercially available image sensor I am aware of is manufactured by Fairchild Semiconductor and consists of a 100-by-100 CCD array containing 10,000 elements. Even though this image sensor provides an excellent picture,

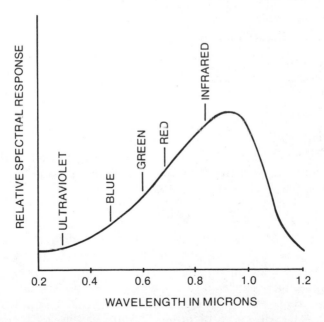

Fig. 5-16. The sensitivity of silicon increases towards the IR portion of the electromagnetic spectrum.

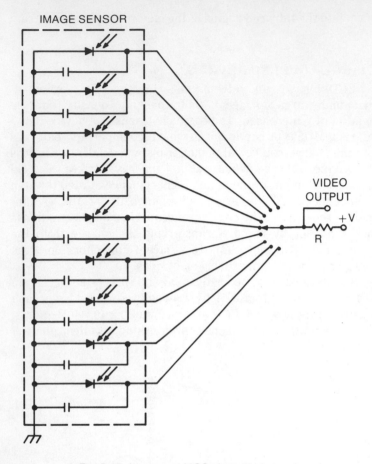

Fig. 5-17. A scanned MOS photodiode array.

it is still far from having the resolution of the CRT vidicon tube. An image sensor must have 163,840 elements (512 by 320) to equal the resolution of most television cameras.

MOS PHOTODIODE ARRAYS

Our second image sensor family, the MOS photodiode array, uses a silicon photosensitive diode as the sensor element. A photodiode, when reversed biased and not under illumination, produces a small leakage current. This so-called *dark current* increases dramatically when light falls on the diode. Basically, as radiant energy falls on the diodes, more current carriers are generated and more current flows. The current flow is thus proportional to the intensity of the radiant energy.

The operation of a scanned MOS photodiode array is shown in Fig. 5-17. The photodiodes are switched in sequence by a "rotary" switch, which in actual use would involve scanning circuits. A capacitor is shown across each diode. These capacitors are not separate components, but rather the inherent capacitances of the photodiodes. When a particular diode is scanned, the capacitor charges to the level of the power supply through resistor R. As the scanning device switches on the next diode, the capacitor discharges through the photodiode it is in parallel with. If no radiant energy is striking the photodiode, the small dark current will only partially discharge the capacitor. With an increase in radiant energy, the capacitor is more fully discharged by the greater current flow. So when the scanning device once again switches to the same diode, an output signal is produced as the capacitor recharges to the power supply level. This video signal is produced by the voltage drop across the resistor, and the greater the capacitor is discharged, the greater the video signal will be. Design engineers call image sensors that operate in this manner *charge storage* CCDs.

There is an alternate mode to utilize photodiodes in a scanning-type image sensor. In this mode, MOS transistors are

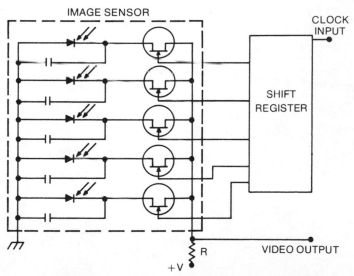

Fig. 5-18. Photodiode array with MOS transistors.

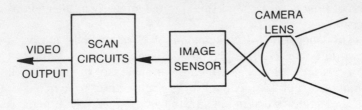

Fig. 5-19. A solid-state video camera.

incorporated as the active devices in the integrated circuit. The photodiodes are still present, but as the source to substrate diodes of the MOS transistors. Figure 5-18 shows an equivalent circuit for this image sensor. The MOS transistors are turned off in sequence by pulses from a shift register, which is indexed by a clock input. Image sensors that include this shift register are called *self-scanning* image sensors.

Solid-state image sensors will, without a doubt, someday replace the more familiar vidicon tubes now used in television cameras. A typical block diagram of such a circuit using image sensors is shown in Fig. 5-19.

Chapter 6

Electroluminescence

The subject of electroluminescence, introduced in the preceding chapter, deserves a deeper study. As the field of solid-state emitters is becoming more widely known, EL panel displays continue to receive attention because they have great potential as an inexpensive and easily fabricated display device that can be made in very large sizes.

Almost all present commercially available EL (electroluminescent) devices use zinc sulphide (ZnS) as the phosphor base material. To this base material different trace elements are added, such as copper. The addition of the element copper produces a green emission in the EL material. Chlorine causes a bluish glow. And manganese produces a yellow color. Research has produced red phosphors as well, but their brightness is still orders of magnitude lower than that of the other EL materials.

The basic structure of an electroluminescent device is similiar to a parallel-plate capacitor, with the phosphor material serving as the capacitor dielectric. One of the two electrodes that form the plates of the capacitor must be transparent in order to emit the light produced by the EL substance. Figure 6-1 shows the basic structure of the EL solid-state light source. To this simple structure an alternating voltage is applied. A high-voltage sinusoidal current is usually required for light emission. The exact operation of the

127

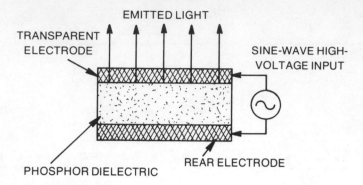

Fig. 6-1. The basic structure of an electroluminescent solid-state lamp.

electroluminescent effects are still not completely understood, but research has also proved that certain phosphors can emit light even if the applied electric field is DC, rather than AC.

Most solid-state physicists accept the theory that if the applied electric field of a normal strength is distributed evenly through the phosphor layer, it will not be sufficient to produce light. It is therefore assumed from observations that there must be *barriers* or local regions of high conductivity within the phosphor dielectric. Within these regions of high conductivity, the applied field is concentrated in the crystals of the phosphor. Some scientists believe that additives such as copper, which are probably present as copper sulphide, produce this high conductivity and thus concentrate the electric field.

There are two main types of electroluminescent light sources—the organic-on-glass and the ceramic-on-metal constructions. The organic-on-glass EL panel as shown in Fig. 6-2A consists of a glass sheet, upon which a layer of transparent tin oxide is deposited. Next comes the phosphor layer and then a reflector layer, which is generally a compound such as barium titanate. Barium titanate is an excellent reflector and also an excellent dielectric with a high dielectric constant. An organic resin is used to bind these layers and materials together. The structure of the capacitor is completed by evaporating a second electrode of metal to the reflector layer. The completed structure can be inexpensively sealed in paraffin wax to exclude moisture. The exclusion of moisture is essential for long life expectancy of the solid-state light source.

128

The ceramic-on-metal electroluminescent light source (Fig. 6-2B) is constructed on sheet steel. Sheet steel lends structural support and also serves as the back electrode. A ground coat of white reflecting material is followed by the

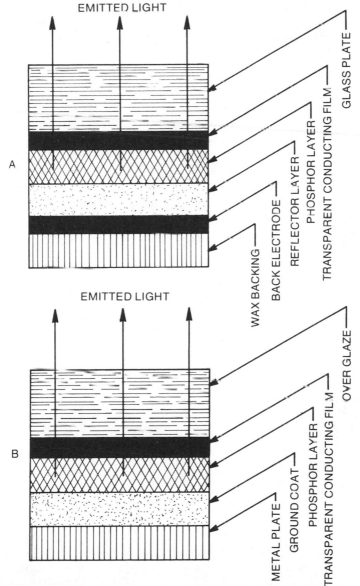

Fig. 6-2. (A) Organic-on-glass EL. (B) Ceramic-on-metal EL.

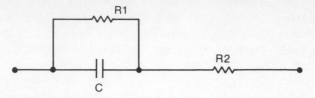

Fig. 6-3. The circuit equivalent of an EL looks like an RC circuit in series with a second resistor.

phosphor layer, which is applied by a vitreous glazing material that also serves as the binding substance. The glazing enamel is fired at a relatively high temperature to insure proper bondage of the layers. A transparent conducting film of tin oxide forms the other electrode and completes the lamp. An overglaze is then used to protect the completed structure.

The ceramic-on-metal EL lamp is extremely resistant to mechanical shocks and can easily withstand higher operating or ambient temperatures than the organic-on-glass. The ceramic-on-metal is also thinner, having a thickness of about 0.76 mm, whereas the organic-on-glass structure has a thickness of 6.35 mm.

The electroluminescent light source responds like a capacitor, having an equivalent circuit as shown in Fig. 6-3. In the equivalent circuit, R1 represents the dielectric losses and R2 represents the electrode resistance. Table 6-1 compares the characteristics for the organic-on-glass ELs and the ceramic-on-metal types of solid-state lamps.

In the table, the efficiency quoted is for maximum brightness. At lower brightness levels the efficiency will, in most cases, increase. In some cases the efficiency may rise as high as 5 lumens/watt. For comparison, a typical tungsten filament lamp has an efficiency of 12 lumens/watt, but almost all of this incandescent light energy is wasted in most

Table 6-1. Comparison EL Devices

CHARACTERISTIC	CERAMIC		ORGANIC	
	A	B	A	B
Voltage	240	350	240	350
Frequency (Hz)	50	400	50	400
Current (mA/in.^{2})	0.125	1.6	0.2	1.6
Brightness (foot-lamberts)	2.5	20	3	25
Efficiency (lumens/watt)	0.8	0.65	1.55	0.70

applications because the lamp is not viewed directly. For example, in a sign using EL devices to display information, the display is viewed directly, requiring only about one percent as much light energy as indirectly viewed projection systems. Almost all the light emitted from the electroluminescent panel is directed to displaying of the information.

By controlled thickness of the EL sources, the operating voltage range can be changed. The operating voltage range usually falls somewhere between 100 and 600 volts. Most EL light sources are presently constructed to operate at either 240V or 350V. It should be noted that the table only applies to the standard green types of electroluminescent displays.

The brightness B of an electroluminescent device depends on the applied electric field and various different equations have been searched to fit the observed characteristics. The equation $B = A \exp(-b/V^{1/2})$ applies over a wide range of values and also seems to agree closely with observed data. Constants A and b are parameters depending on the phosphor used and the exact cellular construction, and V is the applied voltage.

A brightness/voltage curve is shown in Fig. 6-4. The brightness also depends on the operating frequency of the

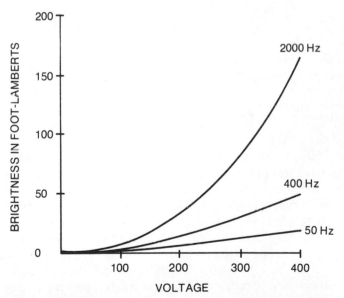

Fig. 6-4. The brightness of an EL depends on both the voltage and frequency of the applied source.

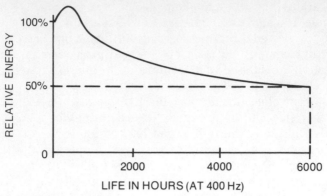

Fig. 6-5. An electroluminescent device has a half life of approximately 6000 hours in use.

lamp. Actually, the EL brightness is nearly proportional to the supply frequency between 50 and 2000 Hz.

Figure 6-5 shows the life expectancy of the standard EL solid-state lamp. Note that there is a tendancy for the EL to rise in brightness near the initial operation life of the device. The decay that follows is roughly exponential in nature. As in other solid-state devices, it is customary to define the life expectancy of the electroluminescent light in terms of how long it takes for the output to reach 50% of the initial value.

From experiment it has been determined that the life expectancy of the EL is roughly inversely proportional to the supply frequency. Interestingly, this observation can be looked upon as meaning that the EL device will operate for a given number of cycles. This given number of cycles is approximately equal to 10^{10}, which is a good-sized number. During the same studies it was also determined that the half-life of the EL is almost independent of the magnitude of the applied voltage. Thus, at a given brightness level, it is desirable to operate the EL panel at its *maximum* voltage tolerance and at the *lowest* possible frequency.

As a rough guide, the following frequencies hold true: In darkness, signs using EL devices should be operated at about 50 Hz. Such signs include exit markers, etc. In moderate daylight, the operating frequency may be increased to about 400 Hz. And in very high ambient light conditions, the figure of 2000 Hz is used to represent the maximum supply frequency.

One of the most important features of EL solid-state devices is their almost complete freedom from catastrophic failure. An EL need only be replaced when its brightness level gradually falls below an acceptable level.

Another feature of the electroluminescent panel was mentioned before, that of having different spectral energy distribution curves for ELs. The curves given are for blue, green, and yellow, plotted with the different phosphors being operated at 400 Hz. One other curve (dashed line) is also given for a green phosphor being operated at 2000 Hz. Above 1000 Hz, the blue emission band of the green phosphor increases rapidly in intensity and overtakes the green band present at the lower frequencies, thus shifting the color toward blue as the frequency is increased. Other green phosphors are known that will remain in the green band even when the frequency is increased. The colors of the yellow and blue phosphors do not change with any significance with an increase of frequency.

Other colors, some even approaching white, can be realized by mixing different proportions of different phosphors together. The only serious drawback to the intermixing of phosphors is a gradual color change during the life of the device, since different phosphors age at slightly different rates. The research into producing other colors, especially that of red, has not been entirely satisfactory. The usual method of producing red is the *cascade excitation* of suitable organic fluorescent materials.

The brightness waveform of an EL device is of a very complex nature. Under laboratory conditions, the rise and fall times for EL lamps are measured over a few cycles of the applied electric field. For lamps which exhibit very low contact resistance (resistance of the electrodes and the actual contact area), the rise and fall times are in the order of a few microseconds. But experimentation has also found that the exact rise and decay times depend on the immediate previous excitation of the EL and on the time intervals between excitations.

The uses of the electroluminescent panel increases every day. The first commercial uses were in applications such as indicators, replacements for light-box indicators (indicators that illuminate a sign from behind by an incandescent lamp), and small-area sources. In general, electroluminescent lamps are not suited to space illumination because of their low efficiency, usually unsuitable colors, and the present size limit to 12-inch square panels.

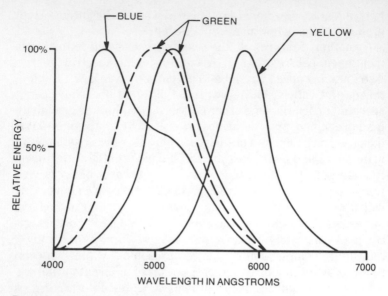

Fig. 6-6. Spectral distribution curves for different EL phosphors at 400 Hz (solid lines) and at 2000 Hz (dashed line).

Because of the ease in which the back electrode can be divided into sections in the organic-on-glass type ELs, many intricately and individually connected light-emitting surfaces can be created. This type of information display is very light, consumes only about 1.5 watts, and is quite stable against shocks. One of the interesting features is that the legend or symbols presented by this type of display are *completely* invisible until a potential of about 350 volts at 400 Hz is applied.

Another display system using ELs is the *100-dot indicator*, so termed because it is made up of a square matrix of one hundred lamps, with each lamp about a ¼-inch square. Obviously, 100 separate lamps are not used, but rather the back electrode is broken up into 100 areas, each with its own electrode connection. There is only one transparent conducting film covering the ELs surface.

One very useful EL application is in numeric and alphanumeric indicator displays. Visibility is excellent in this type of display, where all the indicator segments lie in the same plane. Displays of this nature have been made from ⅜-inch to over 5 inches in height. Indicators smaller than ½-inch are not commercially being made, the reason being one of size, not of any structural problems. If the need arose,

EL indicators smaller than ¼-inch could be readily fabricated. Simple lamps normally use the ceramic-on-metal type of construction, since they are easier and cheaper to fabricate than the organic-on-glass panels.

IMAGE INTENSIFIER

There is another class of special applications well suited to the electroluminescent lamps, which are essentially lamellar in nature and have low current consumption and uniform brightness variation over a wide range of applied voltages. Because of these unusual properties, the EL has found its way into a number of interesting devices. For example, the electroluminescent lamp can be used as an intensifier and converter of radiant energy.

The basic structure of the EL image intensifier is slightly different than regular ELs and is shown in Fig. 6-7. The special construction includes a photoconducting layer, so the intensifier works with X-rays, beta rays, and gamma rays. A

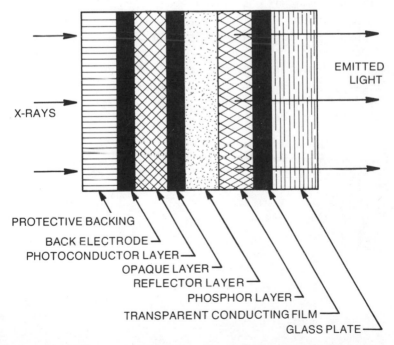

Fig. 6-7. Specially prepared ELs can be used as image intensifiers to convert X-rays into visible light images.

brightness gain of the order of 50 times or more is realized over the conventional fluorescent screen. It is usual to find an optically opaque layer between the EL layer and the photoconductor layer to prevent *light feedback*, which would give increased amplification but at the expense of definition and stability of the image. By using controlled feedback, some amplification increases can be realized, and along with this amplification increase, the image persistence is increased to about 45 seconds after the incident radiation is removed.

A few other special electroluminescent layers can be added to the image intensifier. These include a special phosphor mixture of zinc sulphide activated with both copper and manganese. This ceramic-on-metal EL emits yellow light when a DC potential is applied, and a green or blue light when an AC field is applied.

This special electroluminescent element also has interesting uses as an *image retaining panel*. When the phosphor is used with an applied DC field, the device is sensitive to cathode rays, light rays, and X-rays. When a radiation image strikes the EL device in subdued ambient light, a visible image is produced. This visible image will last for about 30 minutes after the incident radiation causing the image is removed. To clear or erase the panel, the field is removed momentarily, then reapplied. The main uses for this kind of display element is in the location of short-duration laser beams and in the realms of X-ray radiography.

Chapter 7

The Injection Laser Diode

The laser is probably one of the most important recent discoveries in the world of optics. The laser—an acronym for light amplification by stimulated emission of radiation—was first developed using a ruby crystal as the optical cavity and a xenon flashtube as the stimulus, or optical "pumping" source. There are a host of laser techniques, but we are mainly interested in the PN junction laser, usually called the *injection* laser.

BASIC LASER TYPES

Each and every laser source has its own advantages and disadvantages. With the many options now available to the electro-optical designer, a laser system can be readily tailored for almost any practical problem. Techniques range from mode-locking and cavity-dumping, to selection of high-quality materials with linear or nonlinear characteristics. Lasers can use continuous wave (CW) semiconductors and liquid dye mediums, employ exotic optical pumping methods, and achieve high peak-power levels.

The glass or crystal laser makes the optimum choice if high peak power and broad bandwidth are required. The dye laser offers the same features as the solid crystal laser. The comparatively broad bandwidths of these types of lasers are employed to generate ultrashort (less than 10^{-12} second) pulses.

A third class of lasers employs gas as the active medium and operates reliably in the visible region of the electromagnetic spectrum. But gas lasers that operate in the visible portion produce substantially less output power than infrared lasers. For example, the HeCd (helium-cadmium) gas laser produces a relatively small output, but is excellent in use with photoresistive materials employed in making integrated circuits. On the other hand, gas lasers using CO_2 (carbon dioxide) and CO (carbon monoxide) produce very high power levels in the infrared region. These efficient IR lasers are used in welding and in *parametric down conversion* to longer wavelengths.

Crystalline lasers employ mode-locking and cavity-dumping techniques, both of which are relatively new in the optical field. Some crystalline lasers are particularly suitable for the mode-locking method because of their spectral bandwidth (0.0001μ). The solid-glass lasers operate at room temperatures $(20°C)$ in the pulsed (P) mode as opposed to CW lasers. The solid-glass devices are often made into high-power lasers. All gas lasers can use cavity-dumping technology.

Another method of optical pumping is called *chemical* pumping. Optical pumping of all types refers to the use of a primary light source to produce lasing in the affected material. Such primary light sources could be a xenon flash or a separate primary laser. In the latter case, the primary laser acts as the stimulator for the second laser. Chemical pumping also uses an optical pumping source, but the lasing effect is now generated by a chemical reaction in the laser material, which typically involves a fluorescent organic compound dissolved in an appropriate solvent.

The *dye* laser is almost as new as the injection laser diode. Lasing is achieved by optical pumping to stimulate the dye into lasing. Dye lasers are typically operated in the pulse mode, but recently CW operation has been reported. CW operation of a dye laser is carried out by circulating the active medium through the optical cavity and pumping with a CW laser. The following list describes three common dye lasers:

DYE	SOLVENT	TUNING RANGE
calcein blue	ethanol	0.449 to 0.490 microns
fluorscein	alkaline solvent	0.520 to 0.570 microns
cresyl violet	ethanol	0.630 to 0.690 microns

The active molecules in a dye laser fluoresce over a relatively large bandwidth (0.035μ to 0.080μ). Since lasing can occur over most of the bandwidth range of the dye laser, the selection or tuning is possible using such techniques as intracavity gratings, cavity-mirrors, and etalon).

ILD OPERATION

The injection laser diode (ILD) has a radiant-energy producing mechanism similiar to that of the LED. In a forward-biased PN junction, minority carriers are "injected" across the PN junction. Recombination can occur in either of two modes: radiatively or nonradiatively. In the former, radiant energy is expelled.

The choice of material is quite important as it will dictate the photon energy of the ILD. In direct bandgap materials such as GaAs, the photon energy is close to the bandgap energy of the material used in the construction of the ILD. (The first successful ILD was created by injecting zinc into N-type GaAs.) In indirect materials such as GaP, the impurity levels that are involved tend to shift the photon energy to a point below that of the bandgap energy of the material used.

An ILD is a *coherent radiant source* LED, and it is treated as such. Actually, when any LED's radiant energy is coherent, the device is termed an injection laser diode. In construction the ILD must have a very flat junction region, and end mirrors are required (Fig. 7-1). To be a practical ILD, the material used for the construction of the ILD must be of the direct-bandgap family of semiconductors, the device must be constructed in such a manner that an optical cavity is formed, and a region must be formed that will confine the radiation and the injected carriers.

The optical cavity is more precisely known as a Fabry-Perot cavity, which consists of two mirrors or mirror-like surfaces that control the direction of photon flux. In practice the Fabry-Perot cavity is created by cleaving the direct-bandgap material along parallel crystal planes, either of which may be polished to a final reflectivity. The confinement of radiation to this "wave-guide" region is achieved by controlling the dielectric constant (and therefore the index of refraction) to the transverse direction during the growth processes of the semiconductor crystal.

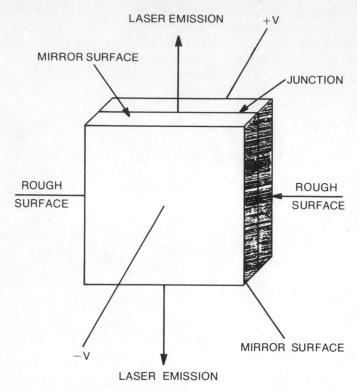

LASER EMISSION   +V

MIRROR SURFACE

JUNCTION

ROUGH
SURFACE

ROUGH
SURFACE

−V

MIRROR SURFACE

LASER EMISSION

Fig. 7-1. The laser injection diode closely resembles the LED.

As stated before, ILDs and LEDs are very similiar in nature. Below the lasing threshold current I_{TH} (see Fig. 7-2), the ILD emits radiation spontaneously and randomly, exactly like an LED. Once sufficient current is applied to the device, more electrons are excited than those which are not excited—a condition called *population inversion*, which is critical for laser activity. For the device to lase, one photon must stimulate another photon after collision with an electron.

The most up-to-date injection laser diodes are of the *heterojunction* (close confinement) type, where the refractive-index differences in the region of the junction are obtained by using layers of AlGaAs and GaAs. The higher bandgap energy of AlGaAs, which is adjacent (parallel) to the lasing region of the GaAs material, also provides for carrier confinement. This carrier confinement produces an important effect—a lowering of the required threshold current density to start lasing in the injection laser diode. Another byproduct is an increase in quantum efficiency.

The single heterojunction ILD (Fig. 7-3) is the most common configuration for close-confinement solid-state lasers, and it will emit typically at around 0.90μ. This ILD is generally operated in the pulse mode with a duty cycle of 0.1%. The peak power of this type of injection laser would range from several watts for single diodes and up to 1000 watts for arrays and modules (Fig. 7-4). At 77°K the close-confinement laser diode can be operated in the CW mode if heat-sinking is employed.

More recently, the double heterojunction laser device has appeared. It has improved radiation confinement, with the important ability to be operated in the CW mode at room temperatures. As of yet this type of ILD is not commercially available.

A very similiar device to the double heterojunction laser is the large optical cavity (LOC) injection laser diode. It will undoubtedly have a duty cycle of about 1% and produce high

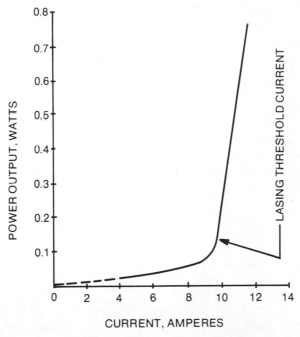

Fig. 7-2. Typical GaAs laser output curve.

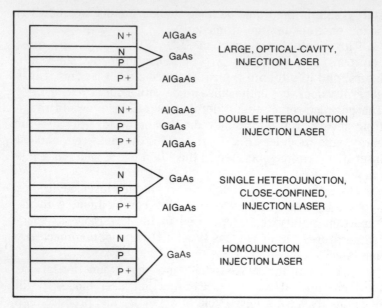

Fig. 7-3. Cross-sections of typical solid-state injection lasers.

output power at relatively high temperatures. In all cases the AlGaAs layer is epitaxially grown.

Tables 7-1 and 7-2 compare parameters between LEDs and ILDs and give a list of materials and their respective wavelengths.

Table 7-1. Comparison of ILD and LED Devices

TYPE	GaAs (LOC) ILD	GaAs (sh-cc) ILD	GaP LED	GaAs LED	GaAsP LED
Emission	0.9μ	0.9μ	0.55μ 0.69μ	0.94μ	0.61μ 0.66μ
Spectral Bandwidth	0.015μ	0.015μ	0.03μ 0.09μ	0.05μ	0.03
Drive current	15A	30A	15 mA	50 mA	15 mA
Mode	pulse	pulse	pulse/CW	pulse/CW	pulse/CW
Pulse Duration	$0.1\ \mu sec$	$0.2\ \mu sec$	unlimited	unlimited	unlimited
Rise time	1 nsec	1 nsec	300 nsec	300 nsec	10 nsec
Output	5W	12W	2.5mW	2.5 mW	·2.5 mW
Power Efficiency	5 – 10%	3 – 5%	0.1% 3.0%	3%	1%

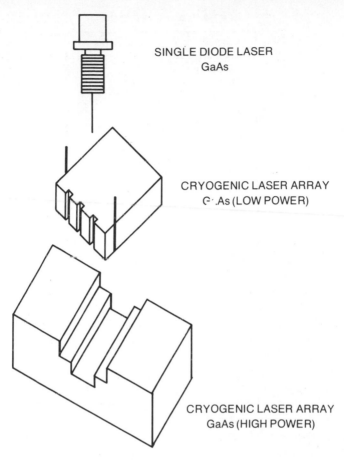

SINGLE DIODE LASER
GaAs

CRYOGENIC LASER ARRAY
GaAs (LOW POWER)

CRYOGENIC LASER ARRAY
GaAs (HIGH POWER)

Fig. 7-4. ILD types.

POWER SUPPLIES

As can be expected, injection-laser power supplies must be specially constructed to produce the required current pulse and to control the duty cycle (on/off ratio). ILDs are generally used in circuits where high pulse-repetition rates are required and the pulse duration is extremely short. The main controlling element is usually a high-speed SCR (silicon controlled rectifier). The pulses must be carefully applied to the ILD since the laser diode is not to be regarded as a rectifier—reverse-bias pulses can destroy or at the least impair the operation of the device. ILDs typically require peak current of up to 100A with a pulse duration of about 200 nsec.

Table 7-2. ILD and LED Materials

MATERIAL	TYPE	WAVELENGTH
GaN	LED	$0.34\ \mu - 0.7\mu$
CuSe-AnSe	LED	$0.40\ \mu - 0.63\mu$
SiC	LED	0.456μ
ZnCdTe	LED	$0.53\ \mu - 0.83\mu$
GaAsP	ILD	$0.55\ \mu - 0.90\mu$
GaP	LED	$0.565\ \mu$
ZnTe	LED	$0.62\ \mu$
ZnSeTe	LED	$0.627\ \mu$
BP	LED	$0.64\ \mu$
GaP	LED	$0.68\ \mu$
InGaAs	ILD	$0.85\ \mu - 3.15\mu$
CdTe	LED	$0.855\ \mu$
InPAs	ILD	$0.91\ \mu - 3.15\mu$
InP	ILD	$0.91\ \mu$
GaSb	ILD	$1.60\ \mu$
InAs	ILD	$3.15\ \mu$
PbS	ILD	$4.3\ \mu$
InSb	ILD	$5.2\ \mu$
PbTe	ILD	$6.05\ \mu$
PbSe	ILD	$8.50\ \mu$

Figure 7-5 shows the typical block diagram of a power source for an injection laser diode. Figure 7-6 is another possible current source for the ILD, where the current is adjustable via the potentiometer across the collector−base terminals of the transistor. A circuit such as this can provide current pulse up to 30A with the +300V supply and 75A with a +600V supply, both single chips and arrays may be operated from this type of power source. The main problem with this type of circuit is that the current-limiting resistor that keeps the current of SCR below threshold holding current, also limits the pulse repetition rate. Figure 6-7 is a simple oscillator

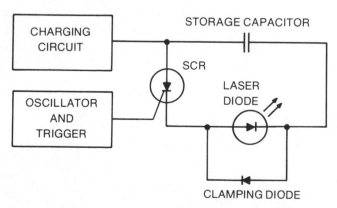

Fig. 7-5. Pulse power supply for injection lasers.

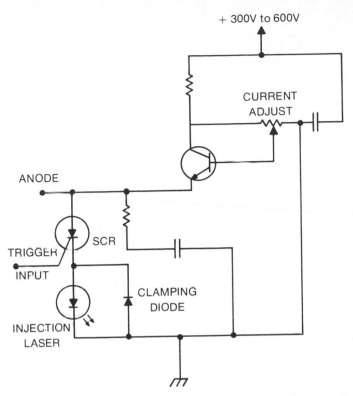

+ 300V to 600V

CURRENT
ADJUST

ANODE

TRIGGER   SCR
INPUT

CLAMPING
DIODE

INJECTION
LASER

Fig. 7-6. Typical laser pulse power supply with provision for controlling current.

circuit which will operate ILDs if they are single chips or stacked chips, but not laser arrays, as the circuit will become unstable with the use of an array load.

APPLICATIONS

There are many applications for the ILD. For example, the ILD can be employed with an image converter to be used at night or in fog as a viewing scope. For measuring distances, the ILD makes an excellent source of radiant energy for *aid-the-blind* devices. Other possible uses include intrusion alarms and communication systems. In many cases, ILDs can replace LEDs.

If you decide to experiment with ILDs—or any other laser, for that matter—be reminded that laser radiation can be extremely harmful to the human eye. Most commercial lasers for experimentation are limited in output power to one

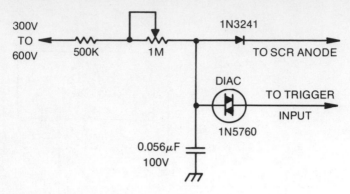

Fig. 7-7. Pulse control circuit for use with power supply in Fig. 7-6.

milliwatt or less for this very reason. The power supplies and associated equipment also may use high voltages, which can be equally dangerous to work with because of the shock hazard.

Chapter 8

Optoelectronic Projects

To fully explore the fascinating realm of photodetectors and photoemitters, you will undoubtedly want to experiment with some of the many circuits in this chapter. Although I must assume that you already have a general knowledge of semiconductors, I have attempted to provide many hints and tips on the construction of the various projects. To this end, this chapter is intended to expand your knowledge and experience with optoelectronic devices such as emitters and detectors, concentrating primarily on the operation of these devices, rather than the other semiconductors that might be used in the circuits. You can also use fiber optics to expand on these projects.

Most experimenters are reluctant to make solder connections or go to the effort of designing printed-circuit boards until they are sure that they want to keep the circuit they have built. This is especially true when experimenting with LED displays that represent a costly investment as compared to other commonplace components such as resistors. It is therefore recommended that you use sockets to lower the risk of damaging the devices. Better yet, use a terminal board like that shown in Fig. 8-1, which has spring-type connections that grip the component leads as they are inserted into the board. Each group of four holes in the terminal board is connected together underneath to form a

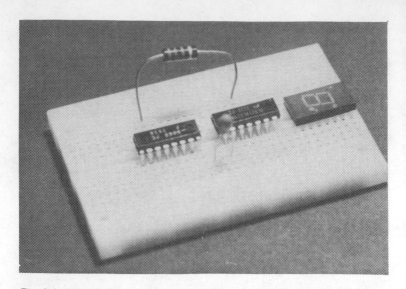

Fig. 8-1. A handy terminal board makes constructing projects quick, safe, and easy. Though more expensive than some other breadboarding techniques, a solderless terminal board protects components from heat damage and makes it a simple matter to change circuit connections.

bus, and the spacing of the holes will accommodate most integrated circuits. Components such as resistors and capacitors can be jumped from one hole to another as the circuit requires, and other direct connections can be made with pieces of wire that have had the insulation stripped off each end. Several manufacturers now make similar boards, but the most widely known at present (and the unit pictured) is made by EL Instruments, Inc., 61 First St., Derby, Conn. 06418.

FAST REACTIONS

This first circuit tests the reaction times of the two players, indicating who is faster by illuminating the LED beside the switch of the faster opponent. Figure 8-2 is the schematic of this circuit, which is straightforward, so there should be little difficulty in constructing this project.

Suppose pushbutton S1 is pressed first. Current will flow through the 470-ohm resistor, through switch S, and through the two series resistors (R3 and R5) and LED-2. At the same time, a positive potential is developed across R5 at the gate of SCR-1, thus turning on SCR-1. The SCR is constructed in such a manner that once current flows (anode—cathode current), the SCR will stay on whether or not current is still applied to the gate.

This half of the circuit now represents a direct current path to ground, so even if S2 is pressed, insufficient current will flow across R4 and R6 in the other leg of the circuit. Thus, no voltage will be developed across the gate resistor and SCR-2 will not be turned on to conduct.

You may have to try different values of resistors for R1 and R2, and for R3 and R4, depending on the type of LED used. A red LED of the GaAsP type should be used as it requires a forward voltage of about 1.8V, while a green GaP LED requires a forward voltage of 3.5V.

DC LIGHT SWITCH

An interesting photoelectric device is the *light-activated SCR*, usually termed a LASCR. Since I'm active in photography as well as electronics, and am somewhat lazy, I'd rather use a gadget than get up. Using the simple circuit in Fig. 8-3, numerous switches can be replaced.

In photography this circuit can be used as the trip circuit for a remote slave flash unit. Merely connect the anode (A) to the positive terminal and the cathode (C) to the negative

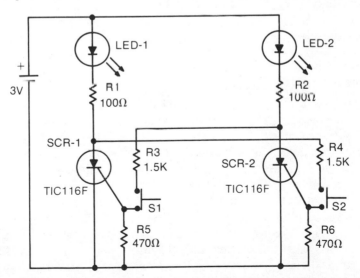

Fig. 8-2. A simple circuit that can be played by two people to test reaction times.

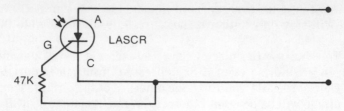

Fig. 8-3. A light-activated, silicon-controlled rectifier can be used as a switch to turn any electronic flash into a slave unit.

terminal of the sync cable from an electronic flashgun. When the main flash attached to the camera is fired, the light burst will trigger the LASCR into conduction, thus firing the slave flash.

If the slave flash is left on, no reset circuit is required. After the slave fires, the voltage potential will decrease on the sync cable until the flash is ready to be fired again. While this is happening, the LASCR turns off as the voltage falls below the holding voltage of the device. Needless to say, the LASCR must be pointed towards the main flashgun.

Instead of a flashgun, other loads can be used if an external power supply is available. For example, a lamp or a relay can be in series with the anode terminal of the LASCR. (General Electric makes a LASCR line called the L8B series.) Pick a suitable LASCR with the proper PIV (peak inverse voltage) so you won't destroy the LASCR. In the case of the remote slave trigger, a PIV of 400 volts is usually required.

INFRARED OSCILLATOR

If an infrared emitter diode (IRED) is used in conjunction with an avalanche transistor you can obtain high-power bursts of infrared energy. With the circuit in Fig. 8-4, the IR pulse durations are a few nanoseconds with an approximate rise time of 10^{-8} sec. The circuit as shown will provide pulse repetition rates of about a few kilohertz.

The IRED I have used was the ME-2 infrared emitter from Monsanto. This diode comes in a TO-5 *stud header* with a low, clear-epoxy lens. The peak emission wavelength occurs at 0.9μ. By slight modifications of this basic circuit, you can change the pulse width (duration) and repetition rate. If you change the 200K resistor in the collector leg of the 2N2041 to a 100K potentiometer and add a series 22K resistor, you can vary

150

the charging rate of the 0.005 μF capacitor. What then happens is that the capacitor is charged through the 200K (or 100K pot with series 22K) resistor until the 2N2041's collector−emitter breakdown voltage is reached. At this point the transistor avalanches, and the capacitor discharges through the transistor and the IRED.

I should mention two points here. First, the infrared emitter is called a IRED because, as discussed earlier, infrared radiation is not visible to the human eye; thus it is not truly light. The term "light" emitting diode is not technically correct here. Second, care should be excercised in the choice of the transistors and the IREDs used.

Consult the manufacturer's specification sheet before substituting for the diode mentioned. This circuit can easily develop current pulses of 15 amperes or more, so the pulse-current rating of the IRED must not be exceeded. (The ME-2 is rated at 25A peak forward current.)

Next check the collector−emitter breakdown voltage of the transistor being used. If the breakdown voltage is too high, too great a current pulse will be developed through the diode. Current through the IRED can be calculated from Ohm's law by finding the series resistance represented by the IRED and transistor and from the breakdown voltage ($I = E/R$). The dynamic impedance of this diode is about 1.3 to 1.5 ohms, and the transistor is approximately 2.4 ohms. The breakdown voltage can be measured across the capacitor with an oscilloscope.

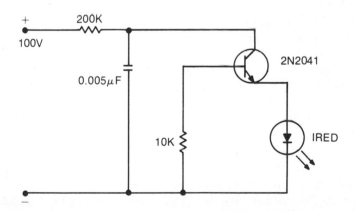

Fig. 8-4. A high burst of infrared energy is possible using avalanche-transistor methods.

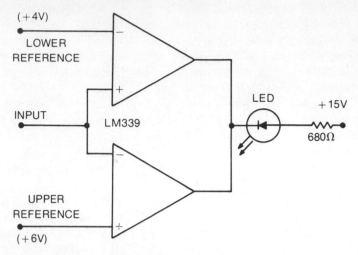

Fig. 8-5. A window comparator can be preset by changing the lower and upper reference voltages.

A way of measuring the pulse current with a fast oscilloscope is to introduce a series precision resistor between the 0.005 μF capacitor and the negative terminal of the power supply (ground). This resistor should be 0.1 ohms, so the voltage reading on the scope, according to Ohm's law, will make the pulse current through the IRED equal to $I = E/0.1$. The pulse width and repetition rate can also be observed across the resistor.

WINDOW COMPARATOR

A "window" comparator is used to indicate whether a voltage is between two established limits. Such a device is useful, for example, in digital circuitry, where a change in voltage can cause misleading results. It can also be used where a voltage is critical and must be kept constant.

In Fig. 8-5, two comparators (LM-339) are interconnected as OR gates. In such a connection, the LED is illuminated when the voltage drops or rises above the limits. In this case the limits are 5V $\pm$1V; that is, if the voltage drops below 4V $(5 - 1)$, the LED will be turned on, and the LED will be also illuminated if the voltage rises above 6V $(5 + 1)$. We can change the window by using different voltages for the lower and upper limit within the specifications of the integrated circuit. A typical LED used here could be an MV-50.

When measuring high voltages, voltage dividers (resistive or electronically attenuated) are used in the input circuit. If the voltage being measured is small, amplifiers may be used to boost the signal. For example, if you need to know if a signal voltage is staying between 3 mV and 5 mV, the upper limit reference voltage could be 5.0V and the lower reference voltage could be 3.0V. The input voltage would then be amplified by 1000 with an operational amplifier. Thus an input signal of 4 mV would be amplified to 4V, which would be within the window of the circuit.

LED STATUS INDICATORS

The following two circuits are extremely simple, but useful. They are also the basis for using LEDs in any circuit It is necessary to limit the current flow through an LED if the LED is to be operated without heating it and possibly destroying it.

Figure 8-6 is used with DC voltages. R1 can be calculated for any LED and any applied voltage as follows:

$$R_1 = (V_{DC} - V_f)/I$$

where R_1 = required series resistor
V_{DC} = applied DC voltage
V_F = rated forward voltage of the particular LED
I = operating current required

In the case were a standard LED must be driven from an AC voltage (Fig. 8-7), a silicon diode such as a 1N914 must be used to protect the LED from reverse voltages on negative alternations of the AC voltage. Here the equation becomes:

$$R_1 = (V_{RMS} - V_F)/2I$$

where V_{RMS} = applied sinusoidal voltage

The 1N914 must always be used if the peak reverse voltage rises above 3V. The 1N914 in this use is called a *clamping*

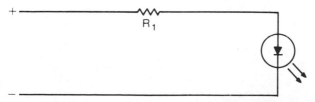

Fig. 8-6. Simple LED indicator for DC voltages.

153

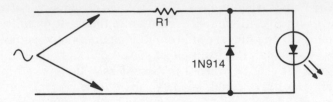

Fig. 8-7. Simple LED indicator for AC voltages.

diode. The factor 2 is needed in the equation because the LED, being a diode, will rectify the applied AC voltage; therefore, only half the current is directed towards light production. If a brightness level is desired to be that obtainable with an equivalent DC voltage, the resistance in series must thus be cut in half.

Of course, in either case a series potentiometer can be added to vary the brightness level of the LED from full-on to full-off. The current-limiting resistor, however, must remain the same to control the full-on current value. The resistance of the potentiometer can be ascertained by calculating the resistance required to achieve minimum current flow (Fig. 8-8).

LED RELAXATION OSCILLATOR

Figure 8-9 is a complementary relaxation oscillator, using an MV-5020 (Monsanto) red GaAsP LED. The 100 μF capacitor provides the necessary feedback to start and maintain oscillation. By increasing the value of the capacitor, the flashing rate decreases; decreasing the value raises the frequency of repetition. The series 1M potentiometer will control flashing rate as well; an increase in resistance will decrease the repetition rate.

I have tried the following transistors and found them satisfactory: 2N2693 as the NPN transistor, and 2N1097 as the PNP transistor. Actually, any small-signal NPN and PNP transistors can be used.

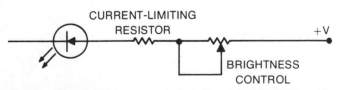

Fig. 8-8. The brightness of an LED can be controlled by a series potentiometer.

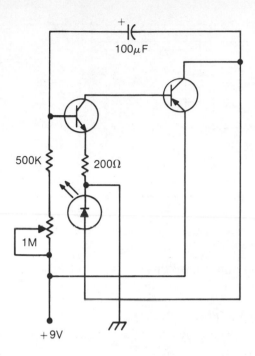

Fig. 8-9. An LED can be pulsed when used as the load in a relaxation oscillator.

IC LED MODULATOR

In this circuit a type 555 integrated-circuit timer is frequency modulated by an external audio signal. This signal is applied to terminal 5, which is the control voltage pin of the IC. This circuit is shown in Fig. 8-10 and can be incorporated as the transmitter in a light-beam communicator.

The choice of diodes depends on the application. If a voltage-controlled flasher is required, a visible LED is required. In the case of a communicator, though, the best is to go to an IRED, since they usually have better control over dispersion in the sense that they usually have a much more narrow beam. Most receivers in a communicator system also incorporate silicon detectors, which are more sensitive to infrared radiation than to light. Most silicon detector devices have their sensitivities centered around 1.1 microns, which is definitely in the infrared.

This type of circuit is a pulse modulator. The timer provides a pulse of approximately 10 μsec in duration every 10

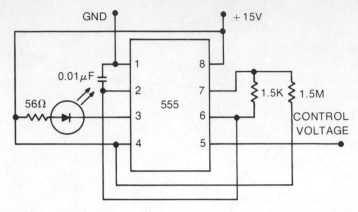

Fig. 8-10. The type 555 timer IC can be used in conjuction with an LED to form a simple transmitter.

msec. If you want to use this circuit as a transmitter, I suggest using Monsanto's ME-60, which is shown in Fig. 8-11.

DISCRETE LED MODULATOR

Figure 8-12 employs discrete transistors and uses an ME-4 IRED by Monsanto. This IRED is a diffused, planar, GaAs type with a peak emission occurring at 0.9 microns. This circuit, though simple, can be modulated as high as 200 kHz. The bandwidth is linear from slightly above 30 Hz to over 150 kHz. Distortion at 1 kHz is 3% or less.

Here again we have an excellent circuit that can be used as a communicator transmitter. Here, and in all transmitters, the use of an external lens to collect and tighten the beam's divergence is quite practical. The relationship of the divergence of the beam, the focal length of the lens, and the size of the beam source is given as

$$\theta = d/f$$
where θ = divergence of the beam in radians
d = diameter of the source
f = the focal length of the lens employed

Fig. 8-11. Monsanto's ME60 IRED is less than one inch in total length and makes a good IR transmitter.

This is easy to say, but it is more difficult in practice. To accurately predict the value of θ, many factors must be considered first. When using an encapsulated diode or a diode with a built-in lens, the encapsulation or built-in lens effectively becomes the source—not the internal chip that actually provides the irradiance. Most lenses are calibrated with reference to their focal length with visible light. In this communicator, as with most, an IRED is used that produces infrared radiation, and this tends to make the calculated focal length longer. To produce efficient collimation of the beam, the source must be placed as close as possible to the collimating lens, and it must be centered on the optical axis as perfectly as possible. Many sources tend to produce a "halo" effect because of random reflections within the structure of the source itself. Here again, problems may arise because much of the irradiance is lost as it occurs outside of the central beam.

I have found that the easiest way to set up the lens/source assembly is to first find the focal point behind the lens. This can be achieved by passing the light from a tungsten bulb 50 feet away through the lens. If a white card is held behind the

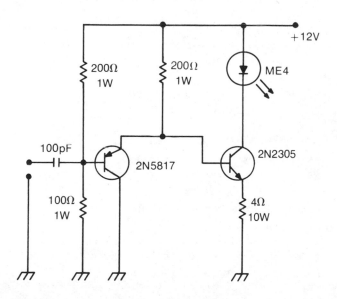

Fig. 8-12. This modulator allows the LED to be modulated with an audio input signal.

157

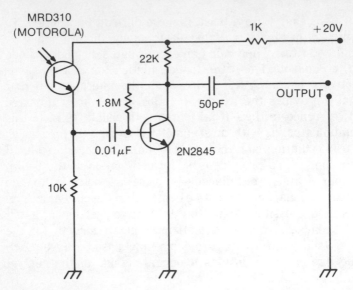

MRD310
(MOTOROLA)

22K

1.8M

0.01μF

10K

1K   +20V

50pF

OUTPUT

2N2845

Fig. 8-13. A receiver circuit can employ a Motorola MRD310 phototransistor as the detector.

lens and moved along the axis, at a certain point the tungsten lamp will be sharply in focus. Use this as a starting point.

When making the communicator (not necessarily this one), mount the transmitter source (or in the case of a receiver, the sensor/detector) at the point you measured behind the lens. If the emitter or detector is mounted with adjustable spacers, final adjustments can be easily made. Needless to say, make the adjustments in subdued light, so as to keep stray light from entering the lens.

PHOTOTRANSISTOR RECEIVER

The circuit in Fig. 8-13 is simple and can be handled as such. But the circuit does have high gain and may be easily influenced by spurious light sources around it. Here, as in the transmitter circuits, a lens can and should be used to focus light upon the phototransistor.

In some cases it may be necessary to optically bias the phototransistor, and this can be easily achieved by placing an IRED near the transistor and operating it at a low level. The IRED can be operated from the same power supply if tapped before the 1K resistor at the positive terminal of the circuit. This IRED can be an ME-4 as used in the transmitter described earlier. A series resistor of 200 ohms should be used with a 25K potentiometer for controlling the brightness of the ME-4. The series 200-ohm resistor will prevent current from rising above 90 mA if you use the power supply with the receiver.

For best possible results, the output from this receiver should be fed to a relatively high-gain amplifier circuit that can drive a speaker directly.

While we are on the subject of amplifiers, the audio input to the transmitter must be several magnitudes greater than that of a simple microphone output voltage. An amplifier should be used between the microphone and the transmitter for best results. The circuits for these amplifiers need not be extensive; they can be one of the pre-packaged modules that many firms have readily available. If you want to build your own amplifier, the type needed for the transmitter should have sufficient gain to drive the circuit with at least 1.5 volts. As far as the receiver goes, the output amplifier should deliver 2 or 3 watts into a 4- to 16-ohm load, which is common for small speakers.

LIGHT-ACTIVATED RELAY

A relatively simple circuit, as shown in Fig. 8-14, can be used as a light-activated relay. In this case, light falling upon

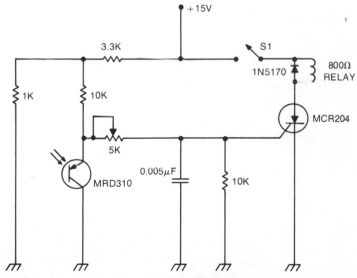

Fig. 8-14. Light-activated relay.

159

CURRENT-LIMITING
RESISTOR

Fig. 8-15. This simple light source can be used with the light-activated relay.

phototransistor MRD-310 maintains the transistor's conduction. As long as the phototransistor is conducting, the gate
of the SCR is held at ground potential. When the light falling
upon the transistor is interrupted, a positive potential is
applied to the gate of the MCR-204 SCR, the SCR fires and the
relay is operated. This circuit can be reset easily via S1. The
0.005 μF capacitor prevents the SCR conducting from spurious
noise or light changes. The same capacitor, in conjunction
with the 1N5170 diode, prevents refiring of the SCR due to the
back-emf from the relay when resetting the circuit. The 5K
potentiometer provides sensitivity control over the circuit.

A simple light source that can be used with this circuit is
shown in Fig. 8-15. If the light source is passed through a room
or across a doorway with the detector on the other side, an
effective intrusion alarm can be designed. The light source
and detector should be powered from batteries so that
operation can continue during a power failure.

BCD DECADE COUNTER

The next circuit can be used for simple counting and
teaches the fundamentals of binary-coded decimal (BCD)
numbers. A BCD decade counter is a circuit that counts
incoming pulses and supplies a running total of these pulses in
the form of binary-coded decimal numbers. In operation, the
circuit in Fig. 8-16 counts from 0 to 9 and then repeats. More
complicated circuits can be achieved by using more than one
counter. Two units will count from 0 to 99, three will count
from 0 to 999, and so on.

I have found that any red LED will work with no problems
as long as the V_F of the LED is under 2.0V. Pulses can be
supplied from a UJT (unijunction transistor) pulse generator
or from any other pulse source that provides positive pulses.

You can replace the LEDs with a BCD to seven-segment,
decoder/driver and use a seven-segment LED readout display.
When using the circuit in this fashion, the possibilities become

160

unlimited. If the pulse source is stable and set to one pulse per second, a timer can be made. In my photographic lab, such a timer is useful in making short exposures and developments.

Figure 8-17 shows a typical unijunction oscillator that can deliver the proper "clock" pulses to the counter circuit. The repetition rate is controlled by the 1M potentiometer and the 0.22 μF capacitor. Different pulse repetition rates are possible by changing this capacitor.

LIGHT-CONTROLLED MULTIVIBRATOR

This circuit is termed as a collector-coupled multivibrator (Fig. 8-18). By varying the intensity of the light incident to the NSL-365 photocell, the photocell's resistance will change accordingly, and the resistance of the photocell determines the operating frequency of this multivibrator circuit.

The 200K potentiometer also determines the frequency of the circuit, and in this manner you can preset the operating frequency under normal light conditions.

The output of the multivibrator is sufficient to drive crystal earphones. Further amplification, via discrete or

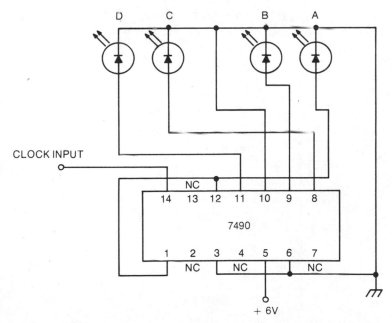

Fig. 8-16. A BCD decade counter uses only one active device, a type 7490 IC.

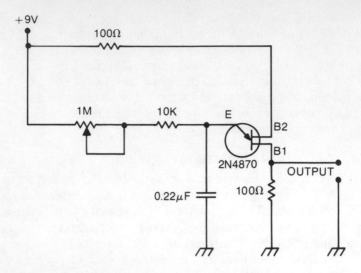

Fig. 8-17. Unijunction pulse generator.

integrated circuits, will allow the circuit to drive a conventional speaker.

To use this circuit as an instrument for the blind or to determine light intensity aurally, a lens assembly would be of benefit. Using a lens would restrict the field of view of the

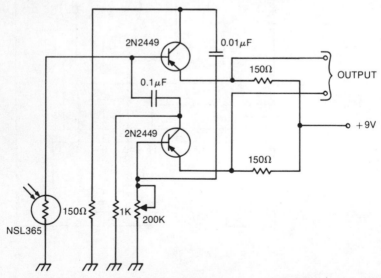

Fig. 8-18. The light-controlled multivibrator's output frequency is a function of the light incident to the photoresistor.

162

photocell and would also focus the light upon it. Here, as in other places through this book, you can modify the circuit in different ways. In this case, try different methods of focusing the light upon the sensor; use different focal lengths and lens apertures. You can try different filtering mediums as well. Needless to say, the lens/photocell housing should be light-tight to prevent extraneous light from falling on the sensor.

ELECTROLUMINESCENT PANELS

Another interesting solid-state light device to experiment with is the EL panel. Like its cousin the LED, the EL panel is immune to catastrophic failure due to vibration and extremes of environment. But where the LED requires a low DC voltage, the EL requires a high AC voltage. A typical EL device will emit radiant energy at a level of 1 to 1.5 foot-lamberts with a 120 VAC, 60 Hz supply.

Commercially available units are made sandwich-style (Fig. 8-19), with a zinc sulfide compound encapsulated between two conductive electrodes. The upper electrode is transparent to the radiant energy and is covered with an insulating plastic film to prevent shocks. The bottom electrode

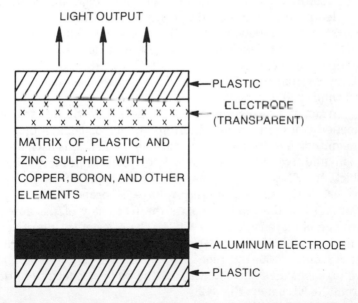

Fig. 8-19. The electroluminescent panel consists of a sandwiched zinc sulphide matrix with added impurities.

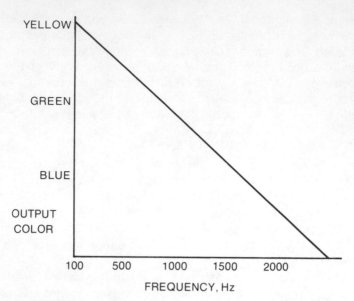

Fig. 8-20. Color shift due to frequency of applied voltage to EL panel.

is typically aluminum and may range from a thin flexible foil to a much thicker, rigid metal sheet. The bottom electrode is also usually insulated with a plastic film. When this sandwich is electrically excited, the phosphor mixture produces a pleasant green glow, though other chemical additives may be added to the zinc sulfide to create different colors. Zinc sulfide compounds of this type are widely used in making the phosphor coatings of the cathode-ray tubes used in television sets and oscilloscopes.

When experimenting with EL panels, you will find that the applied voltage provides different effects, depending upon its magnitude and frequency. When copper chloride is used as the main additive, with a phosphor later about 1 mil (1/1000 inch) thick, the EL panel will glow green if the applied field is 100 Hz at 100 VAC. (The required voltage is proportional to the thickness of the phosphor.) As the frequency of the applied voltage is increased above 100 Hz, the color of the phosphor's glow will shift from green, becoming blue as the frequency approaches 2000 Hz (see Fig. 8-20). Varying the applied voltage changes the intensity of the radiant energy emitted from the EL panel (Fig. 8-21).

Figure 8-22 illustrates a simple driving power supply for EL panels. In this case a separate sine-wave input is required

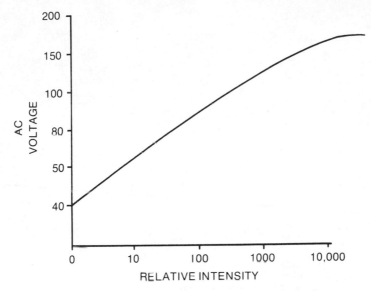

Fig. 8-21. Relative intensity of EL panel with applied voltage.

to modulate the output voltage. Almost any sine-wave generator may be used as long as the generator has no DC in its output.

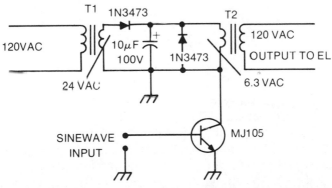

Fig. 8-22. EL power supply requires a sine-wave input to modulate the output voltage. Power transformer T1 supplies a 24-volt AC output that is rectified to produce about 32 volts DC. The transistor amplifies the sine-wave input signal and provides a sine-wave signal to transformer T2, which is a reverse-connected 6.3-volt filament transformer. The 32-volt DC supply is thus converted back into about a 12-volt AC signal before passing through T2. This transformer steps up the voltage, and since the transistor can deliver 12 volts rather than 6.3 volts, the output voltage applied to the EL device can be up to about 240 volts AC. Reducing the magnitude of the sine-wave input to the transistor will correspondingly reduce the AC voltage applied to the EL device.

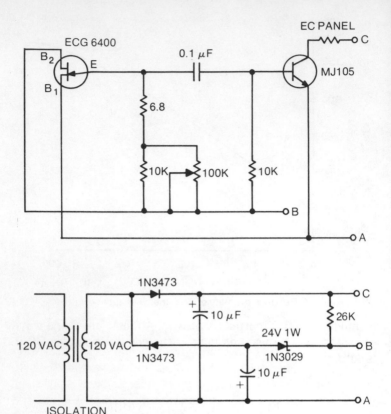

Fig. 8-23. Electroluminescent panel driver contains built-in oscillator.

The circuit in Fig. 8-23 incorporates its own oscillator, thus removing the handicap to those that do not have a generator. The circuit is shown in two parts, one half is the power supply, the other is the modulating oscillators. The 100K potentiometer in the oscillator section controls the output frequency.

Since we are applying an AC field to the EL device, the radiant energy occurs in two bursts per cycle. That is, one burst occurs near each positive and negative voltage peak.

PHOTODETECTOR CIRCUITS

There are numerous photodetectors that are currently available. We will try to cover a few representatives through the general circuit given here, which can be used in more specific problems.

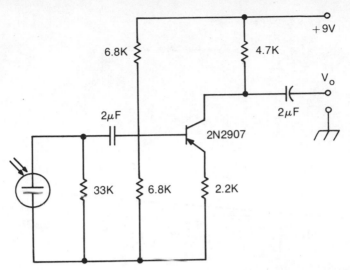

Fig. 8-24. Capacitor-coupled solar-cell detector responds only to pulsed inputs.

Solar Cell Detectors

The first two circuits use *solar cells*—semiconductor devices that generate a photocurrent when exposed to light energy. The first circuit (Fig. 8-24) makes use of discrete devices. This circuit can be used as a pulse detector since the 2 μF capacitors block DC. Quite often, to achieve the desired levels of amplification, additional stages of amplification are required, and these stages may be discrete or integrated circuits.

Figure 8-25 shows a typical circuit that uses an operational amplifier IC. Resistor R controls the gain of the system. This

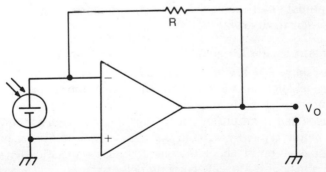

Fig. 8-25. Direct-coupled detector design that responds to average input levels.

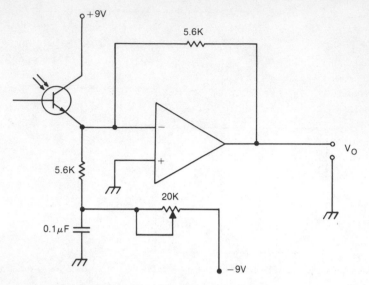

Fig. 8-26. Sensitive detector using phototransistor.

circuit can be used as the receiver in intrusion alarms, but it should be mentioned here that intrusion alarms that incorporate light sources that are not pulses are easier to defeat than a pulse system. I have tested circuits of this type and found that infrared emitters (IREDs) work best as the source. An infrared filter should also be employed since ambient light levels can easily trigger the solar cell into photocurrent generation. Intrusion alarms signal the interruption of the source light falling upon the receiver, so any ambient light that would sustain the photocurrent is undesirable. The output of the IC (709, 741, or similiar op-amps) can be used to drive further circuitry or a high-sensitivity relay.

Phototransistor Detector

Figure 8-26 is a more sensitive receiver/detector than the ones earlier mentioned. In this case the detector is a phototransistor. Here again, an IC (709, 741, or other op-amp) is used as the amplifier. In certain op-amps such as the 709, a capacitor typically around 3.3 pF is required for frequency compensation, so check the manufacturer's specification sheet when in doubt. The 20K potentiometer in this circuit is used to balance DC offset due to ambient light levels.

168

Figure 8-27 shows some typical phototransistors that can be used in this circuit. The two phototransistors are the FPT-100 and FPT-110. The first has a domed filtered cap while the other has merely a flat plastic cover plate. Lenses and parabolic reflectors can be used to greatly increase the sensitivity of the receiver and thus its range. With short distances, the use of such focusing devices is not required. Phototransistors are quite sensitive to ambient light levels and should always be covered with a filter unless they are being used in conjunction with ambient light.

A special variety of phototransistors is the Darlington phototransistor, which incorporates two transistors in a conventional Darlington amplifier configuration. This arrangement increases radiant sensitivity dramatically.

Another new breed of phototransistor is the photo-FET. The phototransistor is relatively slow in response, but the photo-FET is fast. The photo-FET also retains the characteristics of the conventional field-effect transistor.

Phototransistor devices, as with conventional transistors, require biasing if they are to operate as expected. If the base connection is present, it should be used in biasing even though the amplified signal is a radiant one, rather than electrical. This biasing is extremely important in low-level applications because insufficient radiant levels will not properly bias the transistor into conduction. Where no base lead is present, an LED should be employed as the biasing agent, but the emission level of the LED must be carefully controlled so as to not unduly affect the transistor. Basically, even though it is a photocurrent that is developed and amplified, not an electrical signal that is being applied to the base as in a conventional transistor, biasing is still necessary, and the base lead can be used for this purpose.

Photodiode Detectors

Another detector that should be considered is the photodiode. The photodiode is used in one of two different

Fig. 8-27. Typical phototransistors.

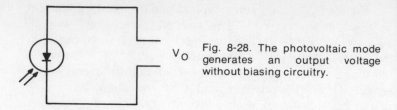

V_O

Fig. 8-28. The photovoltaic mode generates an output voltage without biasing circuitry.

configurations—the unbiased photovoltaic (Fig. 8-28) and the biased photoconductive (Fig. 8-29). These configurations show that the photodiode can be used as either a photoresistor or as a photocurrent source.

In the photovoltaic mode, the photodiode presents the highest signal-to-noise (S/N) ratio, so this mode is usually used to detect low-level DC and low-frequency signals. The high S/N occurs because no load resistors are required.

In the photoconductive mode, a resistor is required and the total system S/N is lowered. But the photoconductive does have its advantages too. It is more sensitive to radiant levels and, since it requires biasing from an external power supply, it can still be regarded as a current source.

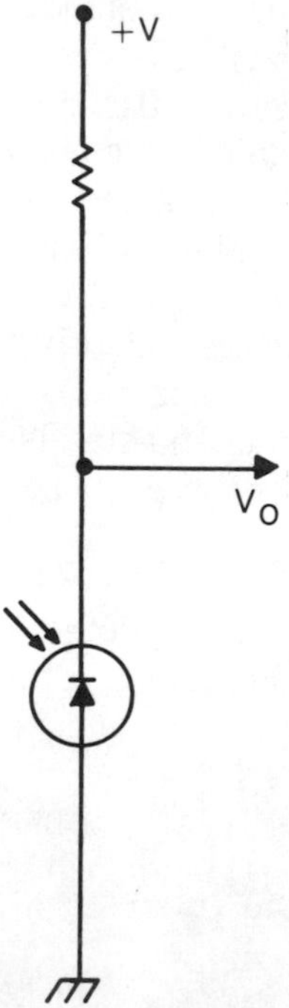

Fig. 8-29. The photoconductive mode uses the photodiode as a variable resistance and so requires biasing.

$+V$

V_O

In either mode, it is the internal capacitance of the diode's PN junction that limits its upper frequency.

A special photodiode, called the PIN photodiode, is operated usually in the photoconductive mode. This diode is ideal for detecting fast pulses from a laser or LED even in relatively strong ambient light levels.

SPECIAL FLASHERS

As in all branches of electronics, where new devices are invented or discovered, new controlling devices spring up. These devices are usually extremely versatile, such as the family of op-amps and timer circuits. In the case of the light-emitting diodes, this new device is the LM-3909 (National Semiconductor) LED flasher, which is a device especially designed to flash LEDs.

Variable Flashers

Turning to the circuit in Fig. 8-30, we have a variable flasher whose rate can be set from 0 to 20 pulses per second. In

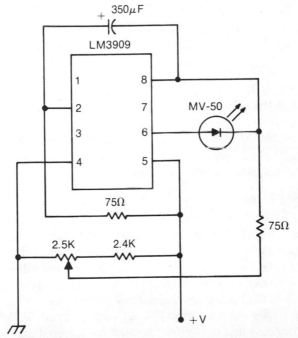

Fig. 8-30. Variable flasher circuit, using the LM3909 device.

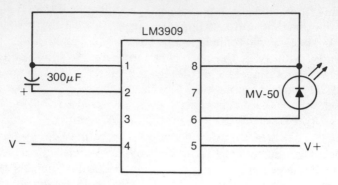

Fig. 8-31. A simple 1 Hz flasher using the LM3909.

this circuit the power supply voltage can be a single 1.5V battery. This is the interesting point about this IC, since most LEDs require a voltage around 1.6V before they emit radiant energy. The LM-3909 is unique among pulse-generating integrated circuits in that it can supply an output pulse whose amplitude is *greater* than the applied power supply. In fact, the flasher can light the LED even with an applied voltage of only 1.0V. How? By electronically discharging the external timing capacitor through the LED in series with the applied power supply voltage so that the two voltages add.

Simple Flasher

In Fig. 8-31 we have a 1 Hz flasher. This type of flasher can be used in the darkroom as a visual time indicator, or perhaps as a transmitter of pulses in an intrusion alarm. Here, as in Fig. 8-30, the MV-50 LED may be used since it requires very little current (it looks like the MV-60 LED shown in Fig. 8-11). The applied voltage should be 1.5V.

Bi-Color Flasher

In Fig. 8-32 we have another of those bi-directional flasher circuits. The applied potential in this case has to be higher (approximately 12V). The 400 μF capacitor determines the flashing rate. With the value given here, the rate will be about 2.5 Hz. One LED is energized as the capacitor charges, and the other when the capacitor discharges. Either discrete LEDs or bi-color LEDs such as the MV-5491 may be used. If different color discretes or the MV-5491 is used, the green diode's anode should be connected toward the 100-ohm resistor at pin 5 of the integrated circuit. This is done because the amplitude of the pulse in this direction is higher, thus compensating for the green LED's lower efficiency.

LIGHT-CONTROLLED XENON STROBE

An interesting device that has been known for a long time in its standard form is the silicon-controlled rectifier (SCR). A special variety of this semiconductor element is the light-activated, silicon-controlled rectifier commonly called a LASCR. Like the more common SCR, the LASCR is a four-layer, three-junction device (Fig. 8-33). The anode and gate connections form two terminals of a PNP transistor. Since there is no base connection or terminal, you can not use a conventional SCR as a transistor. But in the special case of the LASCR, the anode/gate connections may be connected to form a PNP phototransistor.

In the following circuit, any standard xenon flashtube and trigger transformer may be used. I salvaged the trigger transformer and xenon flashtube out of a used photographer's flashgun (the electronic type). Before we continue with the circuit, a few words of caution—the stored charge on the 220 μF capacitor (C1) is dangerous and can easily vaporize the metal tip of a screwdriver.

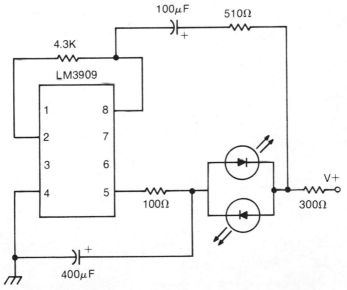

Fig. 8-32. Bi-directional flasher circuit.

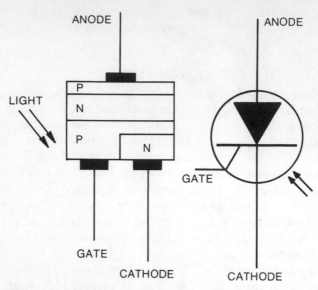

Fig. 8-33. Construction of the LASCR.

If a reasonably sensitive LASCR is used, the light level required to trigger the circuit will be extremely low. The level present from a penlight illumination is usually sufficient to

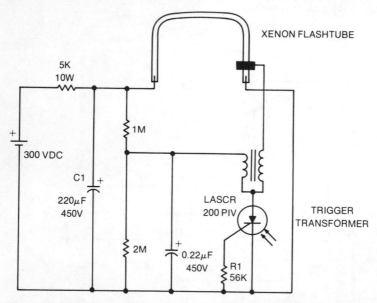

Fig. 8-34. Xenon slave flash unit uses LASCR to remotely trigger flash when main flash unit fires.

activate the LASCR. If the circuit is being used as a remote slave flash unit, you can render the circuit immune to ambient and spontaneous irradiance by inserting a 1-henry choke across the 56K resistor (R1). The coil will prevent triggering from ordinary lights as it will appear as a short circuit to steady-state and slow transients. Yet a very fast pulse, as experienced from the master flash (another xenon flashtube), will bypass the coil and turn on the LASCR. In this case, the coil will represent an open circuit.

LASCR Relaxation Oscillator

The LASCR can also be put to use in a relaxation oscillator circuit, such as in Fig. 8-35. This circuit is a low-voltage oscillator that is light controlled.

The 1 μF capacitor (C1) charges to the level of the supply voltage through the 100K resistor. The 1M potentiometer is placed as a voltage divider, which presents some of the accumulated charge on C1 to the gate of the LASCR. When the turn-on voltage of the LASCR is reached, the device switches on and dumps the C1's charge through the LED. Since the capacitor is now discharged, the LASCR turns off and the LED ceases to light. The process is then repeated over again.

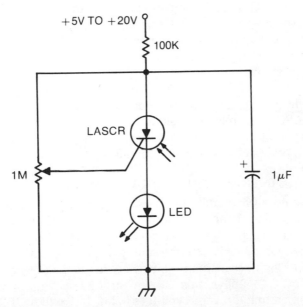

Fig. 8-35. LASCR relaxation oscillator circuit.

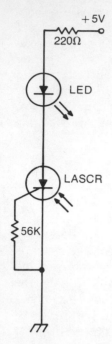

+5V

220Ω

LED

LASCR

56K

Fig. 8-36. The LED in this circuit will light when sufficient illumination turns on the LASCR.

The incident irradiance to the LASCR may have to be adjusted to start oscillation, especially if very low voltages are used. Actually, any voltage from about 5V to 15V may be tried, but with the lower power supply voltages, the ambient light levels will have to be adjusted.

The experimenter with LASCRs may find the following test circuit useful. In Fig. 8-36 the LASCR is normally off. As the light level is increased (incident to the sensitive surface of the LASCR), a photocurrent is generated that will turn the device on. Once in the on state, current flows through the LASCR and the LED goes into conduction.

DIGITAL INTEGRATED CIRCUIT TESTER

Figure 8-37, though not very difficult in construction, can be an excellent bench tool to the person using digital ICs. The circuit can be put to use with a CMOS, TTL, DTL, and even RTL integrated circuits if the supply voltage is positive.

The logic transition point occurs at 1.3V. Any input voltage (V_{IN}) above this causes the LED on that terminal connection to light. Input voltages below 1.3V will not light the LED. A lit LED indicates a logic 1 present. An unlit LED

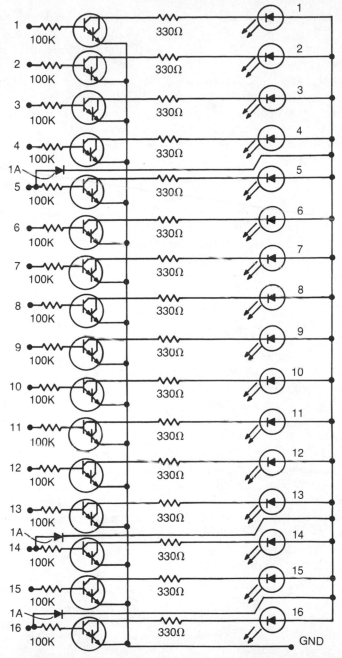

Fig. 8-37. A digital IC tester. The LEDs are type MV-50, the Darlington transistors are type MPSA13 or MPSA14, and the three silicon diodes may be any type rated at 1 ampere.

177

represents a logic 0, a ground pin of the IC, no connection, an open-collector output terminal or an unterminated tri-state output. Brightness will change with the speed of operation of the integrated circuit.

In this circuit, the IC must be in circuit and power must be applied to that circuit. Of course, the big advantage here is that the IC can be tested under actual operating conditions where the logic states of the IC's terminals can be observed. The inputs are numbered from 1 to 16, thus accommodating most IC formats. If you can obtain an integrated-circuit test clip (a clip which makes contact with each IC terminal and has provisions for probe connections on it), testing can be greatly simplified. When using this circuit, connect the terminals up correctly and label the LEDs.

The silicon diodes connected to terminals 5, 14, and 16 are the power supply terminals. They will in no way interfere with the operation of the IC or the IC tester, regardless of which terminal (5, 14, or 16) draws the required power. Since different ICs use different power supply terminals, depending on the number of pins, all three possibilities have been included. Arrange the layout of the circuit and the placement of the LEDs in the physical configuration of the pins of an IC to make it easier to observe the logic states. If you opt for this arrangement for the LEDs, the test clip can be connected permanently to the IC tester. As long as terminal 1 receives the correct positioning, the rest of the circuit will receive power through the diodes.

The circuit will operate correctly with power supply voltages ranging from +4V to +10V. The transistors I have used were Motorola MPSA-13 or MPSA 14. Actually, any NPN Darlington with a beta of 5000 may be used. The Darlington transistors were picked since they represent high gain without having to go to two transistors per branch. Remember to connect the ground connection of the circuit to the grounding point of the circuit being investigated.

ELECTRONIC DICE

The following circuit not only generates the characters 1 through 6 for two Nixie tubes, but decodes and drives the two gas-discharge tubes.

The 7410 integrated circuit is the clock network with the 4 μF capacitor serving as the timing element (Fig. 8-38). The

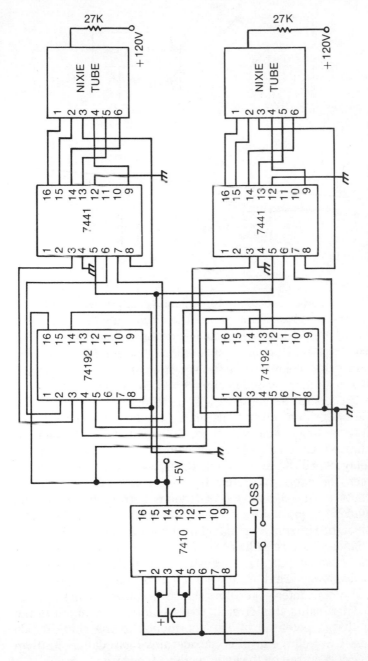

Fig. 8-38. Electronic dice lights up two Nixie tubes to display numerals 1 through 6.

179

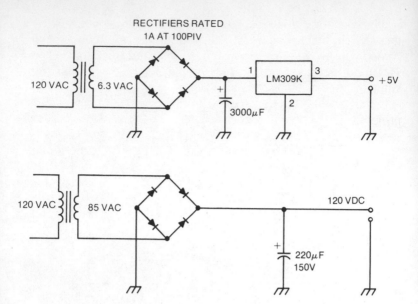

Fig. 8-39. Power supplies for electronic dice circuit shown in Fig. 8-38.

value of this capacitor may be increased to slow the rate of the "toss." The 74192 is a synchronous, reversible, up/down counter that counts the impulses from the clock circuit and delivers a binary-coded decimal character to the Nixie driver. The 74192 is rather complex with its 55 logic gates. Finally, the 7441 integrated circuit decodes the binary number and activates the cold-cathode tube. Outputs 0 to 5 of the 7441 are connected to terminals 1 through 6 of the gas-discharge display. Since the cold-cathode tubes use a separate discharge screen for each character, the 7441 was chosen because it accepts a 1-2-4-8 binary-coded decimal from the 74192 and provides ten mutually exclusive outputs. This IC can directly control the ionizing potential of the indicator display tube.

Since this circuit has two displays for readouts (dice are usually used in pairs), the construction involves twin counting and decoding. That is, the circuit is actually two separate random-character generators sharing a common clock.

When using this circuit, you should pay attention to the fact that a potential of 120V is applied to the cold-cathode tubes. This voltage level is considerably more dangerous than the +5V required by the logic section of the circuit.

180

In operating this electronic dice, the operator presses the toss switch, then releases it. The characters present on the two Nixies will be random. The connections from the 74192 to the 7441 have been set up to exclude characters other than the standard dice configurations.

You should experience no problems constructing this project. Use the two power supplies shown in Fig. 8-39 to supply the +5V and the +120V needed in the circuit.

An all solid-state version of this circuit may be constructed by replacing the type 7441 IC decoder/drivers for the Nixie tubes by type 7447 decoder/drivers that are suitable for driving LED seven-segment displays. The connection scheme would then be like that shown later in Fig. 8-51. The all solid-state version would require only the 5-volt power supply shown in Fig. 8-39.

NEON FLASHER

In any book discussing different types of flashers, whether they be complex or simple, the neon type of flasher is worth mentioning because of its simplicity and its unique way of operating. Two circuits are shown—the first is a single-neon relaxation oscillator (Fig. 8-40), the second is a take-off on the first and is a multi-neon, sequential relaxation oscillator (Fig. 8-41). Both operate in rather the same manner, so we will only discuss the principles behind the first in detail.

In Fig. 8-40, current flows through the 470K resistor and begins to charge the 0.47μF capacitor. The values assigned to the resistor-capacitor pair determine the flashing rate. Therefore we can say that the resistor-capacitor (RC) circuit

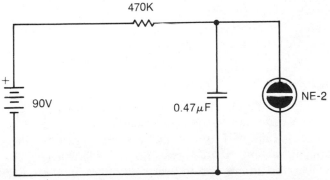

Fig. 8-40. A single-neon relaxation oscillator circuit.

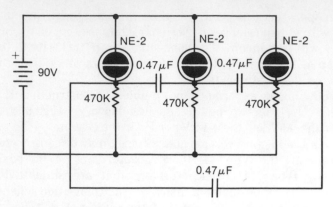

Fig. 8-41. A multi-neon, sequential relaxation oscillator circuit.

is the timing circuit. With the values shown, the flashing rate is approximately 4.5 Hz. The circuit thus has a 0.22 second time constant.

At the beginning of each cycle, current does not flow through the neon lamp. Thus the lamp is effectively out of circuit. In essence, a nonconducting neon glow tube is a virtual open circuit. When the charge on the capacitor reaches the firing voltage of the neon (typically from 60 to 70 volts), the neon tube fires, producing light and becoming a virtual short circuit. This short circuit quickly discharges the capacitor, thus extinguishing the neon glow tube.

In the second circuit (Fig. 8-41), three neon glow tubes are operated sequentially from resistive legs. In both cases you should try type NE-2 neon glow tubes, and the power supply voltage must exceed 90 VDC. In picking the capacitors, remember that the circuit is operating at relatively high potentials, so the capacitors must be rated at the same voltage or higher. The current demand in both cases is very small, in the order of a few hundred microamperes.

PHOTOCELL-ACTIVATED LIGHT

The following circuit has many possible uses. In Fig. 8-42 we have a cadmium sulfide (CdS) cell in the gate circuit of a triac. This CdS cell is not critical in regard to absolute resistance, so just about any common unit will do. The 5K potentiometer allows you to preset the light level required to turn on the triac.

182

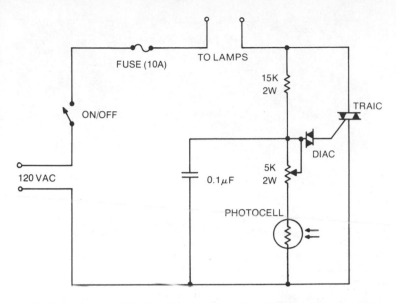

Fig. 8-42. This photocell circuit is used to turn on lights when the light striking the photocell drops below a preset level. The lamps will turn off when the light level increases. The photocell may be any commercially available unit.

As the circuit is capable of handling 1000 watts, heat sinking of the triac is a must; if heat is not removed, it will destroy the triac. Figure 8-43 shows some typical heat sinks

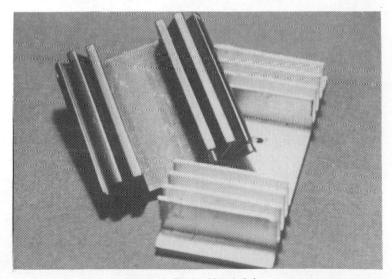

Fig. 8-43. Typical heat sinks.

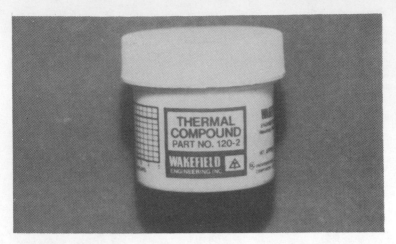

Fig. 8-44. Heat sink compound is essential to insure good heat transfer between the case of the triac and the heat sink.

that are available, and Fig. 8-44 shows a jar of heat sink compound that is used to insure good heat transfer between the case of the triac and the heat sink. Heat sink compound should also be used with power transistors and other power semiconductors that must be mounted on heat sinks.

Terminals labeled with an X are the output connections of the circuit. Lamps up to 1000 watts (place all lamps in parallel) may be connected to this terminal and will light when the ambient light level drops below the preset value.

ONE-ARMED BANDIT

The circuit shown in Fig. 8-45 is an electronic version of the famous "one-armed bandit." The integrated circuits chosen for this circuit include CMOS digital logic units. These ICs are known for their low power consumption—typically a few microwatts per logic gate. The readout of the circuit consists of three LED, common-anode, seven-segment readouts. In the original game, different pictures (usually cherries, oranges, bananas, etc.) are used. Here, different numeric characters are used instead.

To add to the fun of making this construction, which is complex but not overly difficult, an option has been added. This option allows you to add sound effects as well as watch the readout change. This option is shown in Fig. 8-46.

Basically, the circuit operation is as follows. After the normally open switch (denoted *start*) is pushed, three separate oscillators are started, which consist of three gates each. Three decade counters are driven by the output pulses of these oscillators, which operate at different frequencies. As long as the start switch is held closed, the counters will continue to count from 0 to 9 and over again. But once the start switch is returned to its normally opened position, the timing capacitors discharge, the oscillator's input goes from *high* to *low*, and oscillation stops. Since the capacitors discharge at different rates, the three oscillators will stop at different times, approaching the random function of the mechanical bandit. The CD-4026A CMOS decade counters also contain a BCD to seven-segment decoder. This decoded decimal number is fed through the CA-3081 (an array of seven NPN transistors) to drive the LED displays.

In regard to the schematic, a few points should be mentioned. At the connection denoted *option*, the circuit in Fig. 8-46 may be added to simulate the sound of the mechanical wheel stopping in the original. The power source required is the same as the rest of the circuit so you can tap power from the main power supply. The output of the sound-effects generator, which is a decaying 1 kHz tone, can be fed into any audio amplifier.

Pin 15 of each CD-4026A (labeled X, Y, Z) must be connected to the common junction (also labeled X, Y, Z) near the start switch. The three 1N914 diodes (labeled A, B, C) must be connected to pin 11 of each CD-4011A. The number-11 pins are labeled with an A, B, or C. Remember to connect all the points labeled +5V to the power supply and also to ground all points so indicated with a ground symbol.

The LED display can be any common-anode, seven-segment unit, with the recommendation that it is rather large to make the characters readily visible.

No matter how often it is said, it can never be overstated that CMOS integrated circuits are easily damaged or destroyed. Caution must always be observed—especially with these types of ICs. Static electricity is the greatest enemy of CMOS. Never, under any circumstances, remove or insert a CMOS IC into a circuit that is *on* or touch a CMOS IC's terminals with anything other than a grounded instrument. In all circuits involving CMOS ICs, use integrated-circuit sockets like those pictured in Fig. 8-47. Sockets also remove the necessity to solder the integrated circuit directly to a board,

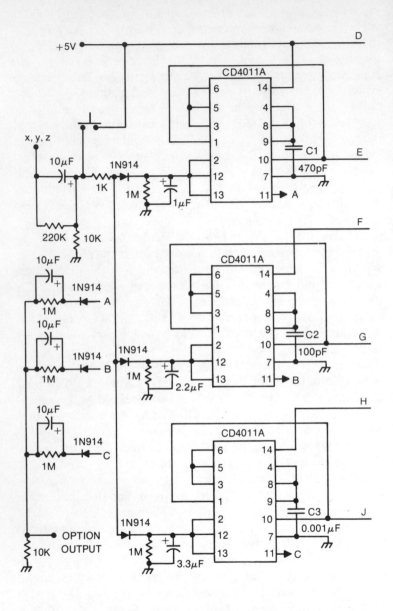

Fig. 8-45. An electronic one-armed bandit.

186

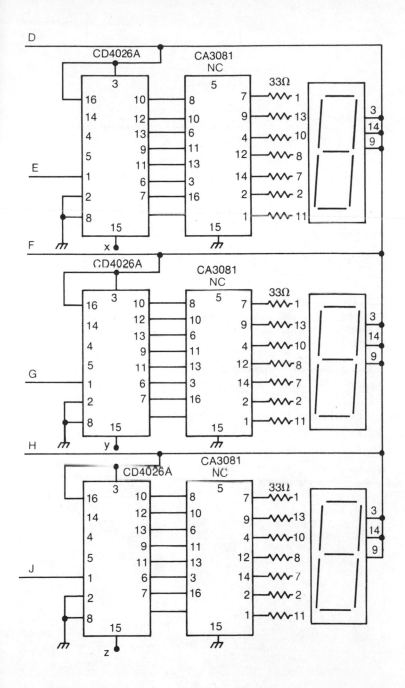

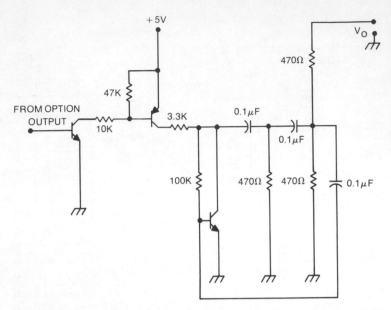

Fig. 8-46. Sound-effect option for one-armed bandit circuit in Fig. 8-45. Output V_O goes to an audio amplifier and speaker to simulate mechanical sounds.

besides making inserting, testing, and removal infinitely easier. LED readouts can also usually be inserted into IC sockets.

On the matter of soldering, use a fine-tip, low-wattage soldering pencil or one of the battery-operated soldering

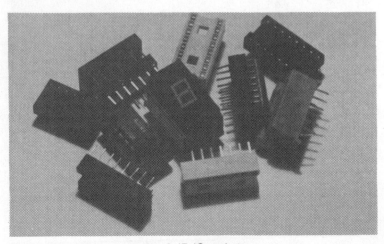

Fig. 8-47. IC sockets.

pencils. The battery-operated units incorporate built-in nickel cadmium, rechargeable battery that can be connected via an adapter to the household line voltage for recharging. This type of soldering pencil is shown in Fig. 8-48 along with a roll of solder. Also recommended for electronic work, especially with ICs and other small lead devices, is resin core 60/40 lead-tin alloy solder; use the smallest gauge possible to minimize solder overflow.

CHARACTER GENERATOR

The following circuit uses a unique digital device—the *programmable read-only memory*. Its uniqueness stems from the fact that it is user programmable; that is, the user can decide what the functions of the programmable read-only memory (PROM) will be. The PROM is an element of the family of *read-only memories*, but the PROM is programmable while ordinary read-only memories (ROMs) are not. The ROM family is called *non-volatile* because if the power is removed from the circuit then reapplied, the stored information remains intact. This memory system can be contrasted with the *random-access memory* (RAM) that has a *volatile* memory. In the volatile case, if the power is removed and then reapplied, the memory will be erased.

Fig. 8-48. Soldering pencil and roll of solder.

Circuit Description

The circuit shown in Fig. 8-49 is a character generator that employs a seven-segment readout as the display device. Using a type 8223 PROM and simple transistor driving circuitry, you can generate the numeric characters, some lower- and upper-case alphabet characters, and some mathematical punctuation. The limitation on what alphabet characters are generated stems from the inability of the simple seven-segment readout to display more advanced or complicated characters.

The ROM integrated circuit remembers bits (*binary digits*) that are organized into *words*, where each word has a given number of bits. For example, the ROM IC we are using in this circuit remembers 256 bits of information. The 256 bits are arranged into 32 words with 8 bits per word. It is this arrangement of bits that sets the number of input (address) lines and output lines that are possible with a given ROM IC.

The input lines are used to select or *access* a specific word from the ROM's memory. The letters A0, A1, A2 etc., usually denote address lines, while the characters B0, B1, B2, etc., stand for output lines. Since the PROM we are using has a memory of 32 words, only 5 address lines are required since $2^5 = 32$. The 5-line address is decoded by logic gates upon entering the integrated circuit.

A ROM with a 256-bit memory must have 256 memory cells. The output lines from the IC are either *high* (logic 1) or *low* (logic 0), and these states are controlled by the programming. Between each memory cell and the internal output transistors, there is a resistive "fuse" or link. If the fuses are left intact, logic 0 occurs. In reverse, if the links are electrically removed (by programming), a logic 1 is possible.

Before we go further to discuss how you program the PROM, we should discuss the character generator circuit in Fig. 8-49. The circuit is based on a single PROM chip, the 8223. I have tried both incandescent and LED displays. If you choose an incandescent, a likely unit would be the model 2100 by RCA. If the LED readout is preferred, a common-cathode type must be used. The transistors can be 2N4123 or equivalent. Switches used in the addressing circuitry are regular spdt types. Remember to supply power to all points so indicated including pin 8 of the IC, the switching network, and of course pins 4 and 12 of the common-cathode LED readout. Table 8-1 gives the

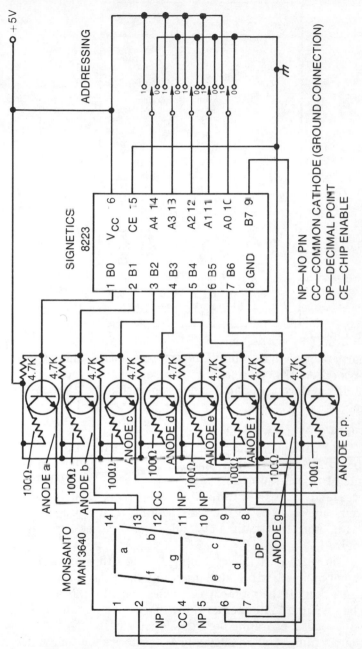

Fig. 8-49. Seven-segment readout character generator.

191

Table 8-1. Character Programming Data for 8223 PROM

DISPLAY CHARACTER	ADDRESS A4 – A0	PROM OUTPUT B7 – B0
0	00000	00111111
1	00001	00000110
2	00010	01011011
3	00011	01001111
4	00100	01100110
5	00101	01101101
6	00110	01111101
7	00111	00000111
8	01000	01111111
9	01001	01101111
.	01010	10000000
-	01011	01000000
=	01100	01001000
A	01101	01110111
b	01110	01111100
C	01111	00111001
c	10000	01011000
d	10001	01011110
E	10010	01111001
F	10011	01110001
G*	10100	00111101
H	10101	01110110
h	10110	01110100
i*	10111	00010000
J	11000	00011110
L	11001	00111000
n*	11010	01010100
o	11011	01011100
P	11100	01110011
r*	11101	01010000
U	11110	00111110
u	11111	00011100

*indicates characters that are only approximations due to the limitations

characters available for different positions of the switching network. As always, a logic 1 represents a high (power supply voltage in this case) and a logic 0 represents a low (in this case ground).

Programming the PROM

Addressing is accomplished by placing the switches labeled $A_4 - A_0$ in either the high ($+5V$) or the low (ground) state. Programming the 8223 is not easy, but it does not necessarily have to be difficult if you are careful and follow the circuit in Fig. 8-50 to the exact detail. In the programming circuit, note that both $+5V$ and $+12.5V$ power supplies are required.

The 8223 PROM is shipped from the manufacturer (Signetics) with all of its outputs at the logic 0 level, which means that all the memory cell fuses are intact. If a logic 1 is to be "written" into memory, the fuses must be removed. It is this process of removing fuses electrically that is called programming. Switch S2 is a two-circuit pushbutton, with one set of its contacts normally closed while the other set is normally opened. S1A and S1B are ordinary toggle switches, while S3 must be a nonshorting rotary with eight positions.

The following procedure must be followed exactly if the proper results are to be expected:

1—Set S1A and S1B to the P (program) position.
2—Select the proper switching order for switches labeled A4 to A0 with respect to Table 8-1 supplied earlier.
3—Set S3 to the desired output (only logic-1 outputs are programmed).
4—Depress S2 for 0.5 sec—no longer as considerable heat is generated by the programming procedure.
5—Allow the IC to cool.
6—Set S3 to the next desired output and repeat steps 4 and 5, using this pattern for all the other outputs.
7—Set the address switches A4 to A0 for the next word.
8—Repeat until all words have been programmed.

By placing the switch S1A/S1B in position T (test), the PROM can be checked wo see if a word has been programmed properly. Leave the addressing switches in the same logic format as the word was programmed, logic 0 will be indicated by a zero meter deflection, and logic 1 will be indicated by a reading of +5V. In this way, each output can be checked to see if the proper logic level is being generated as compared to the table supplied. If you find that logic 1 has not been entered properly (the output is still zero), then repeat the

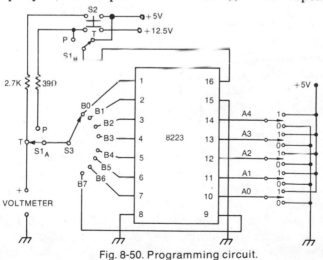

Fig. 8-50. Programming circuit.

programming procedure because the fuse was not completely burned out.

DIGITAL CLOCK

The circuit shown in Fig. 8-51 is considerably more difficult than any previously encountered in this book, and thus must be approached differently. The actual operation of the clock is straightforward—only the physical layout may present a problem. But if care is taken in IC pin connections and wiring, few problems should arise. You are reminded that rechecking of the final wiring is never a waste of time, but rather a saving, if we consider how easy it is to miswire a circuit.

The clock operates as follows. The 120-volt line current is stepped down to 12.6 volts via the centertapped transformer where the low-voltage current is rectified to supply power to the circuit. But a tap-off occurs before the rectification and regulation. This tap-off is fed directly into IC-11^A , which is a *line receiver* wired in a Schmitt trigger configuration. The line receiver can be used as a Schmitt trigger because of its built-in hysteresis of approximately 0.5V. The 8288 integrated circuit (IC-12) consists of two sections, with only the *divide-by-six* section being utilized. The 8288 is really a *divide-by-12* counter and is compatible with the Schmitt trigger, since TTL rise and fall times are available from the 8T14 line receiver.

The 8288 counter is followed by an 8292 *presettable decade* counter. A 1 Hz square wave is generated at pin 5 of IC-13. To count down the seconds and minutes, several 8292 ICs are used in the BCD mode while the 8288 integrated circuits are operating in the divide-by-six mode.

The hours are counted on a twelve-hour basis so that whenever 13:00:00 occurs, IC-6 and IC-7 are strobed to BCD mode, and IC-7 supplies the divide-by-two flip-flop required to provide the "1" in 10, 11, and 12 o'clock.

When setting hours or minutes, *second* counters IC-9 and IC-10 remain reset, while a 60 Hz or a 2 Hz square wave is applied to the CP-1 input of IC-8.

The ICs used in the circuit are as follows. IC-1 through IC-8 are types 8T54 or 7447 IC-6, IC-8, IC-10, and IC-13 are type 8292. IC-7, IC-9, and IC-12 are type 8288. IC-11 is an 8T14, and IC-14 is a type 550 voltage regulator. Switch S1A/X1B must be a 2-pole/4-position, make-before-break type. The readouts can be MAN-1 units or some similar type. The switch positions for S1A/S1B are labeled A for hours, B for minutes, C for hold, and D for run. You set the hours and minutes using positions A and B, stop the clock from running in position C, and leave the switch in position D for normal operation.

For readers interested in a portable digital clock, you can experiment with battery-operated power supplies that provide 12 VDC. A crystal-controlled 60 Hz oscillator is mandatory if precision time-keeping is to be expected.

LED VU METER

In any instrument that uses common meters, the ballistics of the meter are the limiting factor on the response time of the readout. Since all meters possess mass in their coils and stylus, they are inherently slow responding. In the audio world where peak signals are being monitored, the standard meter movement is just not fast enough.

The circuit in Fig. 8-52 uses a series of light-emitting diodes to indicate the amplitude levels of a signal. Each sequential LED from 1 to 9 illuminates fully at 3 dB over the preceding LED, in a 1-to-9 fashion. LED−10 is a peak signal indicator.

The operation of the circuit is as follows. The 10K potentiometer sets the input voltage level to the full-wave rectifier using IC-1. The rectified output is then coupled to 10 parallel voltage comparators. The first nine LEDs are directly driven, while the tenth LED is controlled by a one-shot multivibrator (IC-5) to indicate peaks. One half of IC-2 is used as a voltage regulator to supply a reference voltage. A third regulator, made up of the 2N2222 transistor and diode D11, supplies current to the LEDs. The resistive ladder, composed of 1K and 2K resistors, creates a voltage divider for the 3 dB steps. As the rectified input signal voltage reaches the amplitude level of the reference voltage applied to the plus (noninverting) input of the different comparators, the comparators switch on and light their respective LEDs.

Construction of this circuit is straightforward and should not represent any problems. The following integrated circuits are required: IC-1 is a type 558 and IC-2 through IC-4 are type LM-339. The LEDs I used are MV-50 types. All diodes are type 1N914 or equivalent.

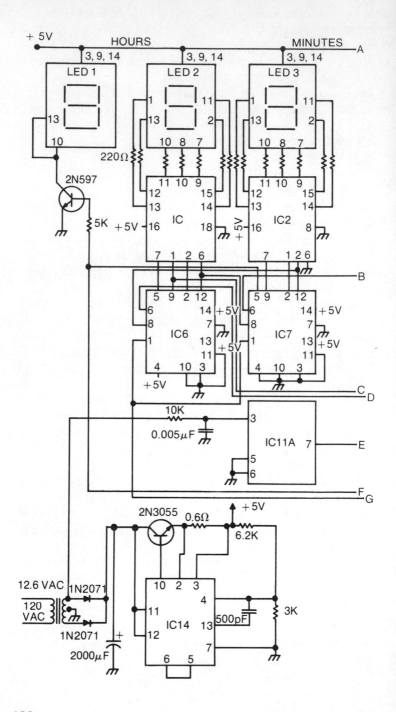

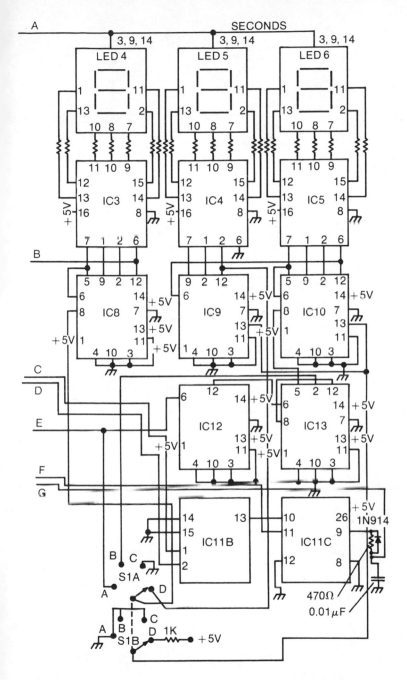

Fig. 8-51. Digital clock circuit.

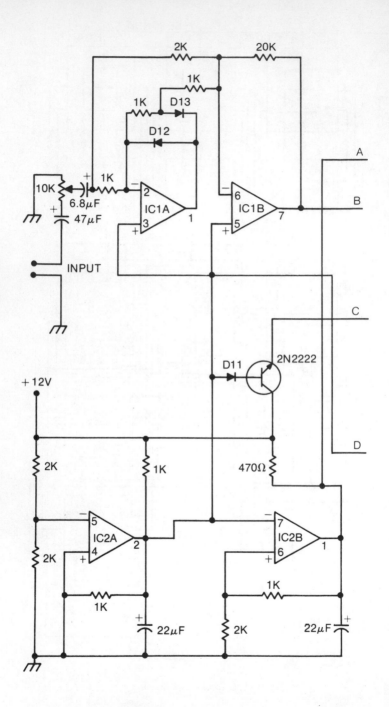

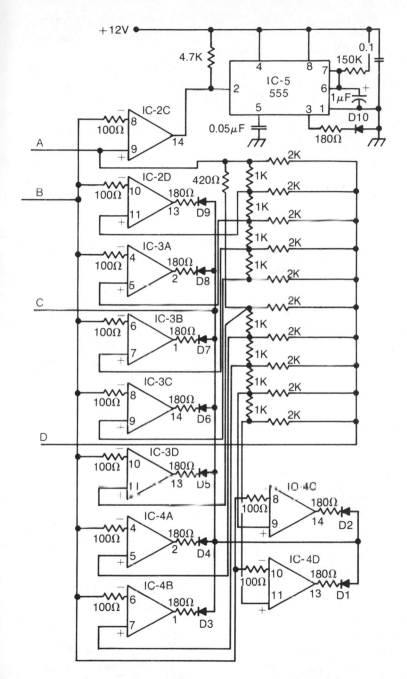

Fig. 8-52. LED VU meter.

When hooking up the power supply connections, remember to connect the +12 VDC to the V_{CC} terminals of the integrated circuits. There are also two other points labeled for +12 VDC in the circuit. The power supply should be able to supply at least 200 mA at 12 VDC. Also remember to connect the ground points of the circuit and the integrated circuits to the ground terminal of the supply.

The 10K potentiometer should be adjusted so that the LED-10 just lights on peaks. The circuit provides a relatively high impedance and thus can be connected across most audio-signal lines without causing any loss of quality in the system.

Since we have stated that the LEDs light every 3 dB of amplitude increase, the total dynamic range of this meter is 30 dB.

MICROCOMPUTER

The following circuit is an actual microcomputer and therefore a shade more difficult than any circuit encountered so far. The rewards of building and using this last project are very high. This circuit also teaches the fundamentals of processor hardware and will allow you to use standard machine-language software (programs).

Perhaps the best place to start is with a short analysis of the circuit and its main building block, the 1802 microprocessor. The basic circuit is shown in Fig. 8-53 and contains 256 *bytes* of random-access memory (RAM)— each byte is 8 bits long and forms part of a larger "word." In this circuit we are using standard 2101 RAM ICs, but actually any RAM or ROM system up to 65,536 (65K) bytes can be handled by the RCA 1802 IC. Another point of interest in regard to this integrated circuit is that a ROM is not required for system operation. It is quite typical of other microprocessor systems that they require a ROM preprogrammed with an operating system.

The 1802 IC has reasonably flexible I/O (input/output) control and can also directly handle program *interrupt* modes—an interrupt is a signal from some input or output device that requires the attention of the MPU (microprocessing unit). The interrupt signal tells the MPU to stop processing its current job and execute the instructions from the I/O device.

200

The 1802 also has facilities for direct memory access (DMA), which means that an I/O device can directly access a memory location. In Fig. 8-54 we have the basic pin-out of the 1802 MPU chip.

Circuit Operation

If we explain how the memory is addressed with this circuit, we will clear up that problem and provide a better overall understanding of the general circuit operation. The MPU we have picked for this circuit contains 16 general-purpose *registers*, with each register capable of holding 16 bits (2 bytes) of either memory addresses or data. The general-purpose registers are labeled R0 to R15. Because we can enter two bytes per register, we label the most significant byte with the number 1 and the least significant byte with 0. We can now speak about the most significant byte of number n as Rn-1 and the least significant byte as Rn-0.

Besides the general-purpose registers, there is an 8-bit register called D. This D register is normally used to move bytes around, but the byte in D can be also used in arithmetic operations that are carried out by the arithmetic logic unit (ALU), which is also part of the MPU chip.

We also have in the 1802 three other registers, each 4 bits long. These registers are labeled N, P, and X and hold the 4-bit number that is used to select R0 to R15. For example, when the value of X is equal to 7, Rx (the register selected register X) will be R7. Here, as always, the high-order byte (most significant) is termed as Rx-1 and the low-order byte is labeled Rx-0. The registers labeled X, N, and P therefore select which general register is to be used for a certain operation.

The general registers can also contain address locations of memory. Briefly, if register R10 contains the data 0054, then the memory location M10 as specified by register R10 would be 0054. When we want to speak of a particular memory, as opposed to a selected memory, we would usually label that memory as M(0054). We could also label a memory as Mx, which stands for the memory location addressed by the general register that was selected by the digit register in X.

Since the basic computer contains only 356 bytes of memory, we can just use the low-order bytes for addressing. In the expanded form, the high-order bytes would then be used to select the memory *page*. That is, the high-order byte would

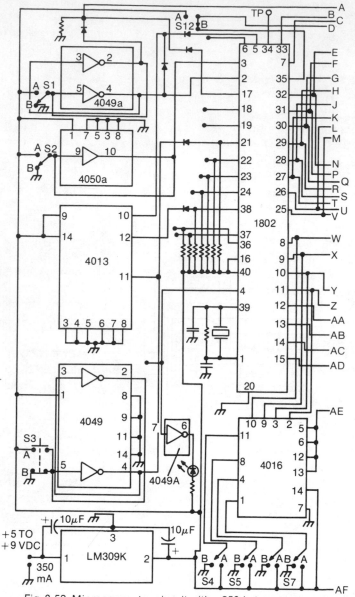

Fig. 8-53. Microcomputer circuit with a 256-byte memory.

select a group of 256 bytes and this group is called a memory page. Since the size of the high-order byte is the same as the low-order byte, we can have 256 pages of 256 bytes each, making a total of 65,536 bytes that could be addressed.

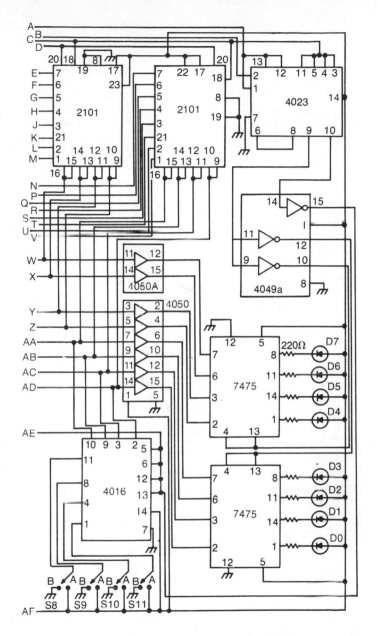

The memory of the computer can contain both instructions to be executed and also data to be processed. Instruction bytes tell the MPU what to do with the data bytes. All 1802 instructions are one byte long and are labeled by

TOP VIEW

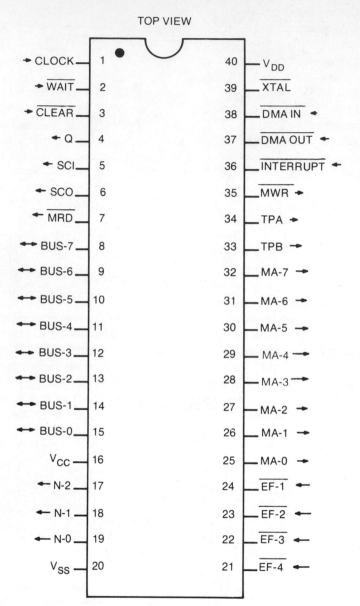

Fig. 8-54. The 1802 microprocessor, showing pin-out names. The arrows show the direction of signal flow.

mnemonics—alphabetic abbreviations that are easy to remember. Table 8-2 gives a complete listing of all possible instruction codes for the 1802 MPU. The table is arranged as follows. The hexidecimal code is given first, then the translation into octal, decimal, and binary. The last column gives the mnemonic for the code and the instruction that is represented by that code.

Continuing with the circuit, any general-purpose register R*n* may be used as the *program counter*—a counter that addresses instruction bytes in memory. Each time an instruction is fetched from memory, the program counter is automatically incremented by one. This automatic incrementation allows the program counter to point to the next instruction to be fetched. Special instructions, called *branch* instructions, allow the program to change the address held in the program counter. This changing of addresses by the program permits *jumping* or *branching* to a different part of the program when desired. The 4-bit digit held in the P register specifies or selects which 16-bit general register will be used as the program counter. Therefore when P = 8, register R8 will be the program counter.

A very important aspect of any computer circuitry is the timing. The 1802 contains a built-in clock. All that is required is an external crystal, one resistor, and two capacitors. For some applications, instead of a crystal being connected to the integrated circuit, an external clock may be used. In our application, the crystal should be around 1.5 to 2.0 MHz.

Using 1-byte instructions, the 1802 requires two machine cycles per operation. During the first cycle, the 1802 always does an instruction fetch, or memory read. Execution of that instruction is always done during the second cycle. One machine cycle is 8 clock pulses in duration, and crystal accuracy controls timing accuracy. During the two machine cycles, two output lines from the 1802, called SCI and SCO, indicate what type of operation the MPU is currently carrying out. The coding on these two lines is as follows.

SCI	SCO	OPERATION
0	0	instruction fetch
0	1	instruction execute
1	0	DMA
1	1	interrupt

Two lines with timing pulses exit the MPU and are called the TPA and the TPB lines. These timing signals are present at

Table 8-2. Mnemonic Instructions for 1802 MPU

HEXADECIMAL	OCTAL	DECIMAL	BINARY	INSTRUCTION (idle)
00	000	0	0000 0000	IJL
01	001	1	0000 0001	LDN load via 1
02	002	2	0000 0010	LDN load via 2
03	003	3	0000 0011	LDN load via 3
04	004	4	0000 0100	LDN load via 4
05	005	5	0000 0101	LDN load via 5
06	006	6	0000 0110	LDN load via 6
07	007	7	0000 0111	LDN load via 7
08	010	8	0000 1000	LDN load via 8
09	011	9	0000 1001	LDN load via 9
0A	012	10	0000 1010	LDN load via A
0B	013	11	0000 1011	LDN load via B
0C	014	12	0000 1100	LDN load via C
0D	015	13	0000 1101	LDN load via D
0E	016	14	0000 1110	LDN load via E
0F	017	15	0000 1111	LDN load via F
10	020	16	0001 0000	INC increment reg. 0
11	021	17	0001 0001	INC increment reg. 1
12	022	18	0001 0010	INC increment reg. 2
13	023	19	0001 0011	INC increment reg. 3
14	024	20	0001 0100	INC increment reg. 4
15	025	21	0001 0101	INC increment reg. 5
16	026	22	0001 0110	INC increment reg. 6
17	027	23	0001 0111	INC increment reg. 7
18	030	24	0001 1000	INC increment reg. 8
19	031	25	0001 1001	INC increment reg. 9
1A	032	26	0001 1010	INC increment reg. A
1B	033	27	0001 1011	INC increment reg. B
1C	034	28	0001 1100	INC increment reg. C
1D	035	29	0001 1101	INC increment reg. D
1E	036	30	0001 1110	INC increment reg. E
1F	037	31	0001 1111	INC increment reg. F
20	040	32	0010 0000	DEC decrement reg. 0
21	041	33	0010 0001	DEC decrement reg. 1
22	042	34	0010 0010	DEC decrement reg. 2
23	043	35	0010 0011	DEC decrement reg. 3
24	044	36	0010 0100	DEC decrement reg. 4
25	045	37	0010 0101	DEC decrement reg. 5
26	046	38	0010 0110	DEC decrement reg. 6
27	047	39	0010 0111	DEC decrement reg. 7
28	050	40	0010 1000	DEC decrement reg. 8
29	051	41	0010 1001	DEC decrement reg. 9
2A	052	42	0010 1010	DEC decrement reg. A
2B	053	43	0010 1011	DEC decrement reg. B
2C	054	44	0010 1100	DEC decrement reg. C
2D	055	45	0010 1101	DEC decrement reg. D
2E	056	46	0010 1110	DEC decrement reg. E
2F	057	47	0010 1111	DEC decrement reg. F
30	060	48	0011 0000	BR short branch
31	061	49	0011 0001	BQ short branch if Q = 1
32	062	50	0011 0010	BZ short branch if D = 0
33	063	51	0011 0011	BDF short branch if DF = 1
34	064	52	0011 0100	B1 short branch if EF1 = 1
35	065	53	0011 0101	B2 short branch if EF2 = 1
36	066	54	0011 0110	B3 short branch if EF3 = 1
37	067	55	0011 0111	B4 short branch if EF4 = 1
38	070	56	0011 1000	NBR no short branch
39	071	57	0011 1001	BNQ short branch if Q = 0
3A	072	58	0011 1010	BNZ short branch if D ≠ 0
3B	073	59	0011 1011	BNF short branch if DF = 0
3C	074	60	0011 1100	BN1 short branch if EF1 = 0
3D	075	61	0011 1101	BN2 short branch if EF2 = 0
3E	076	62	0011 1110	BN3 short branch if EF3 = 0
3F	077	63	0011 1111	BN4 short branch if EF4 = 0
50	120	80	0101 0000	STR store via 0
51	121	81	0101 0001	STR store via 1
52	122	82	0101 0010	STR store via 2
53	123	83	0101 0011	STR store via 3
54	124	84	0101 0100	STR store via 4
55	125	85	0101 0101	STR store via 5
56	126	86	0101 0110	STR store via 6
57	127	87	0101 0111	STR store via 7
58	130	88	0101 1000	STR store via 8
59	131	89	0101 1001	STR store via 9
5A	132	90	0101 1010	STR store via A
5B	133	91	0101 1011	STR store via B
5C	134	92	0101 1100	STR store via C
5D	135	93	0101 1101	STR store via D
5E	136	94	0101 1110	STR store via E
5F	137	95	0101 1111	STR store via F
60	140	96	0110 0000	IRX increment reg. X
61	141	97	0110 0001	OUT 1 output 1

Table 8-2. (continued)

HEXADECIMAL	OCTAL	DECIMAL	BINARY	INSTRUCTION (idle)
62	142	98	0110 0010	OUT 2 output 2
63	143	99	0110 0011	OUT 3 output 3
64	144	100	0110 0100	OUT 4 output 4
65	145	101	0110 0101	OUT 5 output 5
66	146	102	0110 0110	OUT 6 output 6
67	147	103	0110 0111	OUT 7 output 7
68	150	104	0110 1000	not defined
69	151	105	0110 1001	INP 1 input 1
6A	152	106	0110 1010	INP 2 input 2
6B	153	107	0110 1011	INP 3 input 3
6C	154	108	0110 1100	INP 4 input 4
6D	155	109	0110 1101	INP 5 input 5
6E	156	110	0110 1110	INP 6 input 6
6F	157	111	0110 1111	INP 7 input 7
70	160	112	0111 0000	RET return
71	161	113	0111 0001	DIS disable
72	162	114	0111 0010	LDXA load via X and advance
73	163	115	0111 0011	STXD store via X and increment
74	164	116	0111 0100	ADC add with carry
75	165	117	0111 0101	SDB subtract D with borrow
76	166	118	0111 0110	SHRC shift right with carry
77	167	119	0111 0111	SMB subtract memory with borrow
78	170	120	0111 1000	SAV save
79	171	121	0111 1001	MARK push X₁, P to stack
7A	172	122	0111 1010	REQ reset Q
7B	173	123	0111 1011	SEQ set Q
7C	174	124	0111 1100	ADCi add with carry, immediate
7D	175	125	0111 1101	SDBI subtract D with borrow, immediate
7E	176	126	0111 1110	SHLC shift left with carry
7F	177	127	0111 1111	SMBI subtract memory with borrow, immediately
80	200	128	1000 0000	GLO get low reg. 0
81	201	129	1000 0001	GLO get low reg. 1
82	202	130	1000 0010	GLO get low reg. 2
83	203	131	1000 0011	GLO get low reg. 3
84	204	132	1000 0100	GLO get low reg. 4
85	205	133	1000 0101	GLO get low reg. 5
86	206	134	1000 0110	GLO get reg. 6 low
87	207	135	1000 0111	GLO get reg. 7 low
88	210	136	1000 1000	GLO get reg. 8 low
89	211	137	1000 1001	GLO get reg. 9 low
8A	212	138	1000 1010	GLO get reg. A low
8B	213	139	1000 1011	GLO get reg. B low
8C	214	140	1000 1100	GLO get reg. C low
8D	215	141	1000 1101	GLO get reg. D low
8E	216	142	1000 1110	GLO get reg. E low
8F	217	143	1000 1111	GLO get reg. F low
90	220	144	1001 0000	GHI get high reg. 0
91	221	145	1001 0001	GHI get high reg. 1
92	222	146	1001 0010	GHI get high reg. 2
93	223	147	1001 0011	GHI get high reg. 3
94	224	148	1001 0100	GHI get high reg. 4
95	225	149	1001 0101	GHI get high reg. 5
96	226	150	1001 0110	GHI get high reg. 6
97	227	151	1001 0111	GHI get high reg. 7
98	230	152	1001 1000	GHI get high reg. 8
99	231	153	1001 1001	GHI get high reg. 9
9A	232	154	1001 1010	GHI get high reg. A
9B	233	155	1001 1011	GHI get high reg. B
9C	234	156	1001 1100	GHI get high reg. C
9D	235	157	1001 1101	GHI get high reg. D
9E	236	158	1001 1110	GHI get high reg. E
9F	237	159	1001 1111	GHI get high reg. F
A0	240	160	1010 0000	PLO put low reg. 0
A1	241	161	1010 0001	PLO put low reg. 1
A2	242	162	1010 0010	PLO put low reg. 2
A3	243	163	1010 0011	PLO put low reg. 3
A4	244	164	1010 0100	PLO put low reg. 4
A5	245	165	1010 0101	PLO put low reg. 5
A6	246	166	1010 0110	PLO put low reg. 6
A7	247	167	1010 0111	PLO put low reg. 7
A8	250	168	1010 1000	PLO put low reg. 8
A9	251	169	1010 1001	PLO put low reg. 9
AA	252	170	1010 1010	PLO put low reg. A
AB	253	171	1010 1011	PLO put low reg. B
AC	254	172	1010 1100	PLO put low reg. C
AD	255	173	1010 1101	PLO put low reg. D
AE	256	174	1010 1110	PLO put low reg. E
AF	257	175	1010 1111	PLO put low reg. F
B0	260	176	1011 0000	PHI put high reg. 0
B1	261	177	1011 0001	PHI put high reg. 1
B2	262	178	1011 0010	PHI put high reg. 2
B3	263	179	1011 0011	PHI put high reg. 3
B4	264	180	1011 0100	PHI put high reg. 4
B5	265	181	1011 0101	PHI put high reg. 5
B6	266	182	1011 0110	PHI put high reg. 6
B7	267	183	1011 0111	PHI put high reg. 7
B8	270	184	1011 1000	PHI put high reg. 8

Table 8-2. (continued)

HEXADECIMAL	OCTAL	DECIMAL	BINARY	INSTRUCTION (idle)
B9	271	185	1011 1001	PHI put high reg. 9
BA	272	186	1011 1010	PHI put high reg. A
BB	273	187	1011 1011	PHI put high reg. B
BC	274	188	1011 1100	PHI put high reg. C
BD	275	189	1011 1101	PHI put high reg. D
BE	276	190	1011 1110	PHI put high reg. E
BF	277	191	1011 1111	PHI put high reg. F
C0	300	192	1100 0000	LBR long branch
C1	301	193	1100 0001	LBQ long branch if Q = 1
C2	302	194	1100 0010	LBZ long branch if D = 0
C3	303	195	1100 0011	LBDF long branch if DF = 1
C4	304	196	1100 0100	NOP no operation
C5	305	197	1100 0101	LSNQ long skip if Q = 0
C6	306	198	1100 0110	LSNZ long skip if D ≠ 0
C7	307	199	1100 0111	LSNF long skip if D = 0
C8	310	200	1100 1000	LSKP long skip
C9	311	201	1100 1001	LSNQ long branch if Q = 0
CA	312	202	1100 1010	LBNZ long branch if D ≠ 0
CB	313	203	1100 1011	LBNF long branch if DF = 0
CC	314	204	1100 1100	LSIE long skip if IE = 1
CD	315	205	1100 1101	LSQ long skip if Q = 1
CE	316	206	1100 1110	LSZ long skip if D = 0
CF	317	207	1100 1111	LSDF long skip if DF = 1
D0	320	208	1101 0000	SEP set P via 0
D1	321	209	1101 0001	SEP set P via 1
D2	322	210	1101 0010	SEP set P via 2
D3	323	211	1101 0011	SEP set P via 3
D4	324	212	1101 0110	SEP set P via 4
D5	325	213	1101 0101	SEP set P via 5
D6	326	214	1101 0110	SEP set P via 6
D7	327	215	1101 0111	SEP set P via 7
D8	330	216	1101 1000	SEP set P via 8
D9	331	217	1101 1001	SEP set P via 9
DA	332	218	1101 1010	SEP set P via A
DB	333	219	1101 1011	SEP set P via B
DC	334	220	1101 1100	SEP set P via C
DD	335	221	1101 1101	SEP set P via D
DE	336	222	1101 1110	SEP set P via E
DF	337	223	1101 1111	SEP set P via F
E0	340	224	1110 0000	SEX set X via 0
E1	341	225	1110 0001	SEX set X via 1
E2	342	226	1110 0010	SEX set X via 2
E3	343	227	1110 0011	SEX set X via 3
E4	344	228	1110 0100	SEX set X via 4
E5	345	229	1110 0101	SEX set X via 5
E6	346	230	1110 0100	SEX set X via 6
E7	347	231	1110 0111	SEX set X via 7
E8	350	232	1110 1000	SEX set X via 8
E9	351	233	1110 1001	SEX set X via 9
EA	352	234	1110 1010	SEX set X via A
EB	353	235	1110 1011	SEX set X via B
EC	354	236	1110 1100	SEX set X via C
ED	355	237	1110 1101	SEX set X via D
EE	356	238	1110 1110	SEX set X via E
EF	357	239	1110 1111	SEX set X via F
F0	360	240	1111 0000	LDX load via X
F1	361	241	1111 0001	OR logic OR
F2	362	242	1111 0010	AND logic AND
F3	363	243	1111 0011	XOR logic exclusive OR
F4	364	244	1111 0100	ADD add
F5	365	245	1111 0101	SD subtract D
F6	366	246	1111 1001	SHR shift right
F7	367	247	1111 0111	SM subtract memory
F8	370	248	1111 1000	LDI load immediate
F9	371	249	1111 1001	ORI logic OR, immediate
FA	372	250	1111 1010	ANI logic AND, immediate
FB	373	251	1111 1011	XRI exclusive OR, immediate
FC	374	252	1111 1100	ADI add, immediate
FD	375	253	1111 1101	SDI subtract D, immediate
FE	376	254	1111 1110	SHL shift left
FF	377	255	1111 1111	SMI subtract memory, immediate
40	100	64	0100 0000	LDA load advance via 0
41	101	65	0100 0001	LDA load advance via 1
42	102	66	0100 0010	LDA load advance via 2
43	103	67	0100 0011	LDA load advance via 3
44	104	68	0100 0100	LDA load advance via 4
45	105	69	0100 0101	LDA load advance via 5
46	106	70	0100 0110	LDA load advance via 6
47	107	71	0100 0111	LDA load advance via 7
48	110	72	0100 1000	LDA load advance via 8
49	111	73	0100 1001	LDA load advance via 9
4A	112	74	0110 1010	LDA load advance via A
4B	113	75	0100 1011	LDA load advance via B
4C	114	76	0100 1100	LDA load advance via C
4D	115	77	0100 1101	LDA load advance via D
4E	116	78	0100 1110	LDA load advance via E
4F	117	79	0100 1111	LDA load advance via F

pins 33 and 34 of the 1802 MPU. The TPA signal occurs at the beginning of each cycle, and its usual purpose is to control the gating of the high-order address bytes going to the memory. The 1802 addresses the memory by using two bytes; the high-order byte selects the memory page while the low-order byte selects one of the 256 bytes in that page. The TPB pulse occurs at the end of the machine cycle and is generally used to clock bytes going from the RAM memory to the display. During the memory read cycle, the input bytes from the switch keyboard are gated into the RAM.

Reading and Writing

The RAM addresses are sent out on the lines A0 to A7, which are the pins 25 to 32 on the 1802. Eight tri-state, bidirectional bus lines carry data to and from the MPU, RAM, input, and output. The output port in the main circuit consists of output buffers (CMOS 4050 ICs) and latches (TTL 7475 ICs). The two memory control lines, MREAD and MWRITE, control and read and write cycles of the two RAMS. The pulses available at TPA and TPB provide the gating timing pulses as mentioned before. (In cases where you'd like to expand the memory, TPA is used for page selection.)

The 1802 has three output lines, called N0, N1, and N2, that select the I/O device or port desired. In our circuit the N2 line is activated by instruction 6C and goes high. When this signal is sent out, the byte on the bux lines can be written into memory. During the write cycle, the MREAD line will go high when N2 is high, thus allowing switch data to go unto the bus data lines. The information on the bus lines will be stored at the location selected by Rx, and at the same time, this data will be present in the D register.

On the execution of instruction 64, the N2 line will go high and the MREAD line will go low. This will stop any information from the input switches from going out on the bus lines. At the same time the data stored in the memory location selected by Rx is gated out to the display port.

The *load* and *run* lines control the basic operation of the MPU, according to the following table:

LOAD	RUN	OPERATION
L (off)	L	load
H (on)	L	reset
L	H	(none)
H	H	run

During the reset cycle, the TPA and TPB pulses are inhibited. The reset operation sets R0 to 0000, P to 0, X to 0 and Q to 0. In the load mode, a sequence of bytes can now be loaded, starting at address 0000. By setting the bytes on the input switches, where logic 1 is on and logic 0 is off, you can store instructions and data. After each entry is set on the input switches, the switch labeled *input* must be depressed once.

During the loading mode, the 1802 does not do execution, but waits for a low on the DMA-in line. When the DMA-in line goes low, the 1802 performs one memory-write cycle. It is during this cycle that the input data is stored in memory. Register R0 is used to address memory during the DMA-in cycle.

After the input byte is stored at a selected location by R0, this register is incremented by one, thus allowing an automatic sequential loading. The SCI line goes high during the DMA pin cycle so that the control circuitry knows when the input byte has been stored in memory. Operating the switch labeled *input*, produces the low on the DMA-in line. The 1802 responds to this with a memory-write cycle, during which SCI is high. During this cycle the MREAD line goes high, and since the loading switch is high (on), the input byte can be gated to the data bus and stored in the RAM when the SCI and DMA-in lines go high. The computer now waits for the next input byte and loading operation.

Following each DMA-in cycle, the 1802 holds the lines A0−A7 at the address of the byte just stored in the RAM. The MREAD line is held low while in wait for the next input byte. During this cycle the input byte is gated toward the data bus lines, and the output port is activated.

Loading

A sequence of bytes are loaded into the RAM, starting at M0 = M(0000). This is achieved by setting the load switch to the on (high) position, and the run switch to the off position. Next, the input byte is entered by setting the input switches in the proper binary patterns. The switches that are used as the input are labeled S4 to S11, where S4 is the most significant bit of the input and S11 is the least significant bit. When these switches are placed in the positions labeled A in the circuit schematic, they will place a logic 1 on the data bus. When the switches are in the B position, a logic 0 will be generated.

While we are discussing switches, let's consider the other ones as well. Switch S1 is the load switch and represents a logic 1 when in the A position. Switch S2 is the run control, and here as before a logic 1 is generated when the switch is in the A position. S3 is a double-pole/single-throw push-activated switch; when it is depressed a logic 1 is generated. The last switch, S12, is the memory-protect switch, and when it is in the A position, a logic 1 is also generated.

Once the binary code for the data is placed on the switches for input, the input switch is depressed, thus storing the data in the RAM. The value of this byte will now be presented at the output port and will be displayed by the LED readout. This sequence is repeated for each byte required to be placed in memory. The load switch is then set to the *off* position, which places the 1802 into the reset cycle, where R0 = 0000, P = 0, X = 0, and Q = 0. If at this point you want to see the memory, set the memory-protect switch and the load switch to the *on* position. Now each time the input switch is depressed, successive bytes in the RAM memory, starting at M(0000), are displayed.

If an error has occurred in the setting up of the program memory, you can easily change a byte in the RAM. To change a given byte, proceed to the byte immediately *prior* to the one to be changed. Set the memory-protect switch to *off*, place the new byte pattern with the switches at the input port, and depress the input switch one time only. The new byte will be displayed at the output port, and it will also be stored in the RAM at the location following the byte at which the computer was stopped.

Execution

To start the execution of a program that has been loaded into memory, set both the load switch and the run switch to the *off* position. Then set the run switch to the *on* position, which resets the computer by resetting the program counter (P) to 0000. Once the 1802 is reset to operate starting from M(0000) forward, the program will be executed sequentially until the run switch is placed in the off position. During execution, make certain that the memory-protect switch is not activated.

Increasing Display Capabilities

Now that we have discussed the operation and nature of the basic circuit, we are ready to increase the display

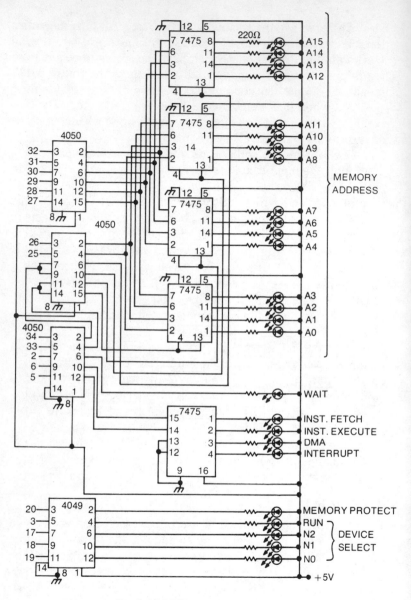

Fig. 8-55. LED binary display.

capability of our system. Figure 8-55 is a circuit that will allow observation of both the addresses currently in use and the status of the computer. The LED labeled A15 to A0 indicate the current address, where A15 is the most significant bit of the most significant byte of address, and A0 is the least significant

212

bit of the least significant byte. The remaining LEDs indicate the status of the computer.

All pin numbers referred to on the incoming lines are pin numbers of the 1802, except pin number 20 of the CMOS 4049 integrated circuit. This line must go to pin 20 of the two RAMs.

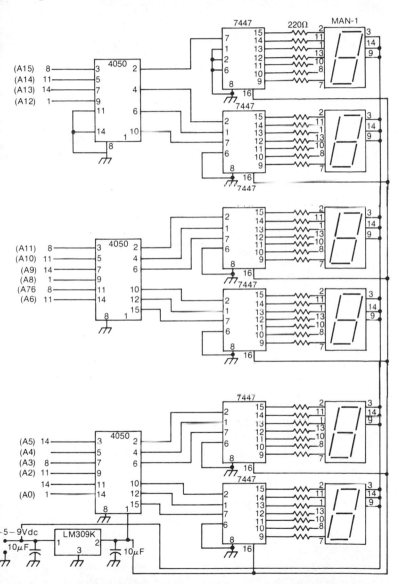

Fig. 8-56. Octal display circuit for displaying addresses.

213

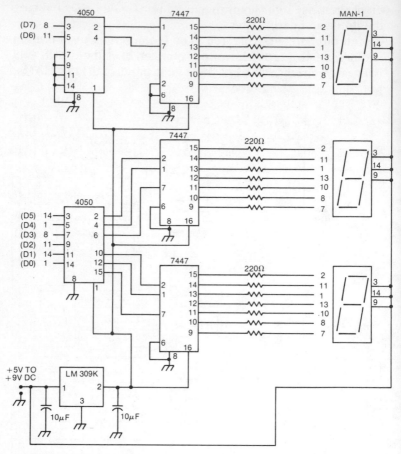

Fig. 8-57. Octal display circuit for displaying data bus information.

Here, as in all other circuits now being presented, the circuit is connected without disturbing any of the original lines of the main circuit.

In the event you want to use the octal display circuit (Fig. 8-56) for the addresses, the circuit in Fig. 8-55 should still be used. A common problem that programmers run into is setting the computer into a loop. The octal display is changing too fast to watch the addresses during actual execution. This problem can be more easily recognized by examining the LED display to see if it is forming a pattern that is the same over and over again, which occurs if the computer is stuck in a loop.

Figure 8-56 shows the circuit for displaying the addresses in actual octal code on seven-segment displays. Because the first circuit (Fig. 8-55) displaying the addresses incorporates the proper enabling and latching circuitry, the octal display circuit is tied directly into it. The incoming lines refer to the pin numbers of the TTL 7475 integrated circuits in Fig. 8-55. The pin numbers also have the lines labeled as A5 to A0, so that you should have no difficulty in finding the matching pins in Fig. 8-55. That is, the line labeled A15 in Fig. 8-56 connects with pin 8 (A15) of the first 7475 IC in Fig. 8-55.

Figure 8-57 is a second octal circuit that allows the computer operator to see the data bus in octal rather than binary. Here again, seven-segment LED readouts are used. The incoming pins are also labeled with the code D7 to D0, where D7 is the most significant bit, so that the pins can be easily found in the main schematic. In all cases, the connection point should be as close as possible to the pins of the driving IC.

Chapter 9
Designing
With LEDs

This chapter is presented for those wishing to experiment with light-emitting diodes in circuits other than the ones given in this book. For this type of experimentation, you will need to familiarize yourself with more of the optoelectronic properties of the LED. A general introduction to the emission phenomenon was presented in Chapters 1 and 2, but this was intended primarily to acquaint you with the basic properties of LEDs, not with the more technical design information.

EMISSION CHARACTERISTICS

As mentioned earlier, the emission of radiant energy from an LED is best described by the semiconductor energy-band theory, and the energy bands change with the type of semiconductor material used. The most common material used in the manufacture of LEDs is the group of gallium-based materials including gallium arsenide (GaAs), gallium arsenide phosphide (GaAsP), and gallium phosphide (GaP). The energy bands of these materials are rather narrow, thus producing a monochromatic emission consisting of a narrow band of radiation wavelengths.

The energy bands of the various semiconductor materials also affect the electrical characteristics of the optoelectronic devices, particularly the forward voltage and forward current that these devices operate at. The required forward voltage, as would be measured across the LED with a voltmeter, is due to the required electric field needed to produce the emission of visible or infrared energy.

An electric field, in the form of an external forward-biasing voltage, is applied across the PN junction of the light-emitting diode. The conduction mechanism is such that the electric field excites the majority carriers, which happen to be electrons. The electrons that gain enough energy cross the energy-gap from the valence band to the conduction band, then return to the valence band. It is during the transition from the N-side conduction band to the P-side conduction band that the electrons give up energy in the form of phonons (heat) and photons (light). The energy released equals the energy absorbed during the transition from valence band to conduction band. The amount of energy released is determined by the size of the energy gap (E_g), and the radiation emitted directly comes from the electrons within the depletion region formed between the two sides of the PN junction.

The electrical characteristics of a light-emitting diode are related to the energy gap as well as the photon emission characteristics. For example, the conduction threshold or "knee" point on the forward-current/forward-voltage (I_F/V_F) curve in the forward-biased direction (see Fig. 9-1) occurs at approximately 1.0V for IR emitters, 1.3V for visible red, and 1.8V to 2.0V for yellow and green light-emitting diodes. The brightness of the emitted radiation is directly

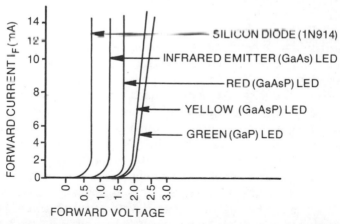

Fig. 9-1. Typical I_F/V_F curves for various LEDs as compared with a silicon diode.

217

proportional to the operating current flowing in the forward direction.

As a semiconductor material, gallium compounds have several important advantages over silicon and germanium. Typically, gallium materials exhibit a lower reverse-leakage current, the forward-current below the knee point is lower, the thermal noise is definitely lower in gallium, and gallium has a very high carrier mobility. Of course, the single, most important advantage of gallium materials—especially from the standpoint of light-emitting diodes—is the ability of gallium to generate light directly from electron flow.

ELECTRICAL CHARACTERISTICS

The reverse breakdown characteristics of light-emitting diodes are not controlled, since the quality of light emission is the first and primary consideration. Reverse-diode breakdown voltages range typically from 5V to 20V; however, the reverse voltage is generally specified as being 3V minimum, which is done to insure device protection.

If a silicon device is subject to junction damage, the silicon will often continue to perform adequately because of silicon's inherent annealing capability. But when junction damage occurs in a light-emitting diode, the result is usually a "softening" of the knee, a flattening of the I_F /V_F curve. The damaged device may continue to operate, but performance will be less than satisfactory and an early failure may occur.

Light-emitting diodes can be damaged in ways other than electrically abusing them. Thermal energy is a great enemy, along with mechanical shock and stress. LEDs generally have a 1-mil gold wire bonded to one side of the semiconductor chip. This wire is usually surrounded with an epoxy-type material. When thermal energy (heat) is applied to the LED in whole, the epoxy, the wire, the semiconductor chip, and the outside casing and leads all expand at different rates. Thus, if too rapid an application of heat is applied, the results are similar to that of a mechanical shock to the gold wire. This can lead to an early failure, if not immediate breaking of the bond contacts or the wire itself. Never apply too great a heat or use temperature cycles with LEDs. The semiconductor material has a tendency to degenerate at elevated temperatures, but epoxy which is the main material used for modern encapsulation, can melt.

Reverse conduction is another area to watch. Too high a current level at the avalanche voltage will cause the light-emitting diode to dissipate excessive power, resulting in thermal buildup and junction degeneration. Adequate current limiting can never be overstressed. As far as forward current goes, watch for pulses from switching elements, and of course watch the applied voltage. A regulated power supply will keep the voltages more constant in the circuit.

BASIC CIRCUITS

The following circuits describe ways to drive the LED properly. Remember when replacing an incandescent lamp with an LED that the LED is current-dependent, while the incandescent lamp was rated only in terms of voltage.

Basic DC Circuit

In Fig. 9-2, you will need to know V_F and I_F, which are found in the specification sheet for the particular light-emitting diode. Here, as in all circuits where current-limiting resistors are used, keep in mind power ratings. The value of current-limiting resistor R_L is found by the equation

$$R_L = (V_{CC} - V_F)/I_F$$

Active-Low Drive Circuit

In Fig. 9-3, a single NPN transistor is used to drive the LED. The LED lights when the transistor collector is *low* (conducting). Here we find the value of R_L by

$$R_L = (V_{CC} - V_F + V_{CC(SAT)})/I_F$$

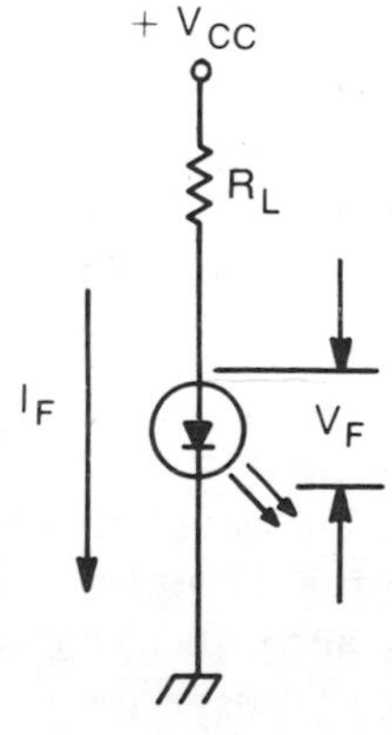

Fig. 9-2. Basic DC circuit.

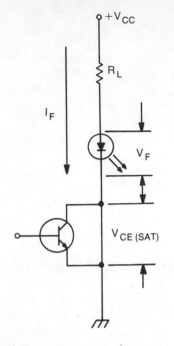

Fig. 9-3. Active-low drive circuit lights
LED when transistor is turned on.

Active-High Drive Circuit

In this type of circuit (Fig. 9-4) a single NPN transistor is
used in such a manner that the LED lights when the transistor
collector is high (not conducting). The NPN units picked
should have a $V_{CE(SAT)}$ of approximately 0.4V when in
conduction. The formula for RL is

$$R_L = (V_{CC} - V_F)/I_F$$

AC Operation

Light-emitting diodes should be operated in the forward
direction only. Therefore the LED circuit must provide
reverse-voltage protection if the applied voltage could exceed
the maximum reverse voltage V_R of the LED (see Fig. 9-5).

VISUAL CONSIDERATIONS

There are other considerations that include the human
observer. Human vision is highly subjective and is affected by
various factors, such as whether the radiation is an *area* or
point source. There is also the viewing distance, the color of
the source, and of course the visual acuity of the observer.

220

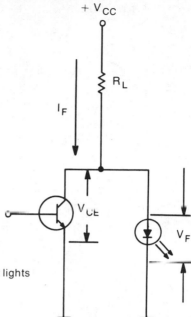

Fig. 9 4. Active-high drive circuit lights LED when transistor is off.

An observer with perfect vision (20/20) can discern objects having dimensions that transcribe angles as small as two minutes. To the observer, this source will be considered the smallest area source viewable. An object transcribing the 2-minute angle is in the order of ⅛-inch in diameter when placed 17 feet away. Any object either smaller or farther away would be viewed as a *point* source, rather than an area source.

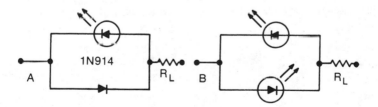

Fig. 9-5. For AC operation, the LED must be protected from reverse voltages, which should never exceed about 3 volts. In (A) a 1N914 diode, or equivalent, is used for protection, with the LED conducting only during the half-cycles that forward-bias the LED. In (B) a second LED accomplishes the same protection and provides light during the alternate half-cycles. Besides using these circuits in AC applications, they can also be used in circuits where voltage polarities are unknown or where the polarity could reverse.

ENCAPSULATION DIAMETER

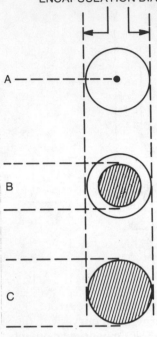

Fig. 9-6. Whether a light source appears as a point or area of light depends upon its diameter and distance from the observer. A diffuser over the LED chip increases the apparent diameter of the source. A true point source (A) has no diameter. A partially diffused source (B) has a larger apparent diameter but may still appear to have a point source at its center. A fully diffused source (C) looks most pleasing and has the largest effective diameter.

The formula

(threshold distance) = 1718 × (light source diameter)

gives the distance at which a source loses its area sensation as seen from the position of the observer.

It should be pointed out that evenly diffused area sources are generally more pleasing to the human eye than high-intensity point sources. Figure 9-6 shows pictorially the effect as seen by the observer of a point-source LED (A), an unevenly diffused LED (B), and an evenly diffused LED (C). Both B and C are considered to be area sources, though the unevenly diffused is sometimes referred to as partially diffused.

CONTRAST RATIO

The degree by which an observer "distinguishes" an object or source is a function both of time spent looking and of the contrast ratio. Contrast ratio is defined as the difference in luminance between an object and its background. Mathematically, contrast ratio = $(L_S - L_B)/L_B$ where L_S is the source luminance and L_B is the background luminance, both usually measured in foot-lamberts.

It has been found that after an observer has focused on an object for a period longer than about one second, the time factor becomes negligible, so the contrast ratio remains the deciding factor in seeing an object. Studies have shown that the minimum value of contrast is a ratio of 10. Thus, if the background luminance is known under the ambient illumination level, you can then calculate the value of minimum acceptable luminance required for the source LED to produce the minimum required contrast ratio.

Color

In certain cases, different colored LEDs may be required to produce equal brightness. Since light output from an LED is basically a function of forward-current flow through the PN junction, equal brightness can be achieved by adjustment of current flow, as in Fig. 9-7. You could adjust the LED current level without checking specifications, but to insure that too high or dangerous a current stress will not happen, you should, at the least, check the specifications for maximum current.

In some cases, the manufacturer provides a curve with the LED, giving the current versus luminous intensity. It should be noted, though, that these adjustments of brightness are based on the interpretation of the observer, whose eye changes its sensitivity with the wavelength of the visible radiation. Thus we have to set the brightness in photometric terms, whereas IR emitters use radiometric terms to describe their brightness.

Besides color choice, you also have different beam patterns. On the whole, IR emitters have a narrow beam, while visible units have a wider viewing angle.

Figure 9-8 can be used for plotting the color of different LEDs. Both the response of silicon and the human eye is given for reference.

REPLACING INCANDESCENT LAMPS WITH LEDS

LEDs are used in great quantities for the replacement of incandescent lamps in places such as computers, printed-circuit boards, and electronic equipment (Fig. 9-9). These solid-state lamps are generally used for status indicators. Their function would include indication of power present, yes/no verification, and on/off tell-tales.

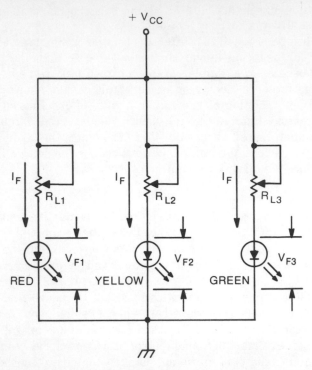

Fig. 9-7. Potentiometers $R_{L1} - R_{L3}$ may be adjusted until all three LEDs have the same apparent brightness. Then the exact resistance value may be measured across the potentiometers for each LED in question.

Incandescent lamps draw large amounts of power and generate considerable thermal energy. This heat generation can deteriorate lamp sockets, structural materials, insulation elements, and the circuits themselves. The high degree of heat generated can even be considered quite hazardous in many cases. The LED runs cooler, uses less power, and has the great advantage of a longer life expectancy, thus requiring less maintenance.

In all cases where incandescent structures are being exchanged with solid-state devices, the absolute maximum ratings must be observed, especially forward current I_F and reverse voltage V_R. Protection must be supplied so that these ratings are not passed. The following must be also considered: polarity reversal, voltage transients, and inductive surges from coils.

In this discussion we will consider Fig. 9-10. (A) is a circuit that can be used in applications with a DC supply voltage equal

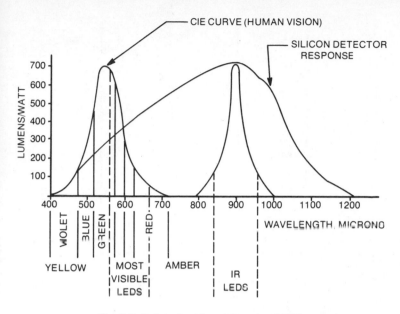

Fig. 9-8. Color chart for comparing LEDs.

Fig. 9-9. A collection of LEDs designed for insertion in printed circuit boards. (Courtesy Hewlett-Packard.)

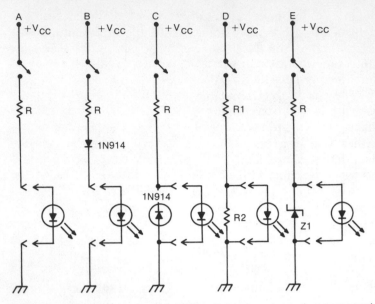

Fig. 9-10. LED circuit examples. The switches may be real or represent other switching circuits.

to or less than the V_R maximum rating of the light-emitting diode. If the LED is positioned in reverse, no damage will occur because no prohibitively high current flows since the V_{CC} does not exceed the V_R maximum. If transient voltage spikes appear on the power supply line, positive-going spikes cause the I_F to increase, but no damage will occur if the proper light-emitting diode is chosen with respect to peak current I_P ratings. Many LEDs with a rather low I_F rating can have a high I_P rating, with their magnitudes approaching several amperes. Negative-going spikes, if they are less in amplitude than the V_{CC} of the circuit, will merely reduce the I_F. But if the negative-going spike is greater than $V_{CC} + V_R$, reverse current I_R can become very large and damage may result. For applications were high-amplitude negative-going spikes are encountered, I recommend the use of circuits (B) or (C).

The V_{CC} in circuits (A) through (C) can be half-wave, full-wave, or battery-supplied DC, provided the peak voltage does not exceed the V_R maximum rating of the light-emitting diode being chosen. An LED used in these circuits can be damaged if plugged into the circuit in reverse if the supply voltage is greater than the V_R maximum ratings.

226

In (D) we have a circuit with an additional resistive element, R_2, whose function is to limit the voltage drop to the V_R rating of the LED in use. This circuit also supplies protection against damage from negative-going spikes of an amplitude greater than $V_{CC} + V_R$.

The circuit in (E) can protect the LED against incorrect polarity as well as voltage spikes of virtually any amplitude. The value of the zener's breakdown voltage is chosen to be less than the V_R maximum of the LED being used, but greater than the V_F of the same LED. When no LED is in the circuit, the zener conducts with a breakdown voltage less than V_R. An LED in reverse polarity is not stressed because the voltage applied across its terminals is less than its V_R maximum rating. Negative-going voltage spikes greater than V_{CC} force the zener into forward conduction, holding the reverse voltage across the terminals of the LED to no more than one volt.

The circuits in (D) and (E) may be used with AC as well as DC if the proper component values are chosen to limit V_R and I_F to safe values.

MATHEMATICS OF EMITTERS AND DETECTORS

Since most LEDs are used in conditions where the observer is human, measurements must be made in reference to the human eye. We thus use photometry to evaluate LEDs. The basic unit of photometry is the *lumen* (lm), which is used to describe the luminous flux radiated from visible objects and emitters. Unfortunately, lumens only describe the *total* flux emitted—without reference to how much of the projected flux is actually being *observed*. So here we have to consider flux per unit solid angle.

The unit of solid angle is called the *steradian* (sr). The quantity of flux thus being observed would be measured in lumens per steradian. One lumen per steradian is termed one *candela* (cd)—a unit replacing the older unit, *candle*. Thus an emitter that produces one lumen per steradian has a luminous intensity (I_V) of one candela.

In regarding LED parameters, the most common terms are the foot-lambert (fL) and the millicandela (mcd). The foot-lambert is a unit of intensity per unit area, called luminance (L_V). Thus we have the equations:

$$I_V = L_V A/\pi$$

where I_V = luminous intensity of emitter in cd
L_V = luminance of emitter in fL
A = area of emitter in square feet (ft^2)

and

$$I_V = L_V A$$

where I_V = luminous intensity of emitter in cd
L_V = luminance of emitter in cd/m^2
A = area of emitter in square meters (m^2)

One more term is necessary to complete our picture of measuring. This term is called *luminous incidence* (E_V). At one time this was referred to as *illuminance*, but the parameter it measures is still luminous flux per unit area incident upon a surface from an emitter or source. If the distance from an emitter to the surface of incidence is sufficient, the incidence will vary inversely as the square of that distance.

$$E_V = I_V / d^2$$

where E_V = luminous incidence at surface in lm/m^2
I_V = luminous intensity of the emitter in cd
d = distance from emitter to surface, in meters

If the distance is in feet, the incidence will be lm/ft^2, where one lm/ft^2 is termed the *footcandle* (fc).

When the radiant energy of an emitter is incident to a detector, the output current, termed the photocurrent (I_p), can be used with the calibration factor (responsivity):

$$E_V = I_P / R_E$$

where E_V = luminous incidence at detector in lm/m^2
I_P = photocurrent from detector in μA
R_E = incidence responsivity of detector in μA/lm-m^2

MEASURING LUMINOUS INTENSITY

When measuring emitters, the typical detector to use is the silicon photodiode, since these diodes exhibit very stable characteristics and possess a low temperature coefficient. Thus, with this information you can now calculate the luminous intensity of an emitter such as an LED even if the emitter—detector distance is unknown. To do this, you merely pick two arbitrary reference planes, using the "ten-diameter" rule, which states that the distance from emitter to sensor must be ten times greater than the diameter of the emitter or detector, whichever is greater.

By using two arbitrary reference planes, you can develop two simultaneous equations that will produce a value for the intensity of the emitter (see Fig. 9-11). Now $I_V = d^2/R_E (I_P)$, so at position 1,

$$I_V = (D_1 + X)^2 /R_E (I_{P1})$$

and at position 2,

$$I_V = (D_2 + X)^2 /R_E (I_{P2})$$

Therefore, by setting the two equations equal and eliminating X, we obtain

$$I_v = \qquad (D_2 - D_1)^2$$
$$R_E \quad \times \quad \frac{(I_{P2})^2}{(1 - \sqrt{I_{P2}/I_{P1}})^2}$$

where I_{P2} and I_{P1} = photocurrent of detector in microamperes (μA) at positions 1 and 2

R_E = detector responsivity in μA/lm-m^2

D_1 and D_2 = distances in meters (m) between arbitrary planes of reference.

I_v = luminous intensity in candelas (cd)

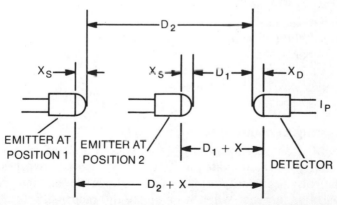

Fig. 9-11. Positioning method used to determine luminous intensity and irradiance. Two sets of measurements are made with the emitter at two different positions.

Measuring Irradiance

You can also calculate the irradiance (E) from an emitter having a given intensity at different distances from the emitter by the inverse square law. If the emitter and detector are in a vacuum or separated by a completely transparent medium, then $E = I/D^2$, where D is the separation distance. But in general this is not the case, so a transmittance factor (T) is added to the equation, making $E = TI/D^2$. The transmittance factor ranges from unity (clear) to zero (opaque).

Measuring Quanta and Flux

In physics, the energy of a single quantum is determined by

$$hv = hc/\lambda$$

where h = Planck's constant (6.625×10^{-34} joule-seconds)
v = frequency of the radiant energy
λ = wavelength of the radiant energy (microns)
c = velocity of light (2.998×10^{14} microns/second)

Now the radiant flux per unit wavelength is $\Phi\lambda$, and the radiant flux in a small increment of wavelength $d\lambda$ is $\Phi_{E\lambda}\ d\lambda$ watts. The radiant flux in this narrow wavelength band may be converted to a rate of flow of quanta:

$$N = \lambda\Phi_{E\lambda}\ d\lambda/hc$$

where N is the number of quanta per second.

Usually in discussing photodetectors, you evaluate the device in terms of the flux incident on the photosensitive area of the detector. You can specify the flux as the number of quanta per second at some wavelength, the radiant flux in a wide or narrow band of wavelengths. We could also use luminous flux and sometimes even flux density (flux per unit area).

Measuring Responsitivity

The term *responsitivity* (R) is used to describe the sensitivity of a photodetector, and this is normally expressed as the ratio of the output current (or voltage) to the input flux in watts or lumens. When we indicate the responsitivity at a particular wavelength, $R(\lambda)$, we are describing the spectral response of the device. If $R(\lambda)$ and radiant flux $\Phi_{E\lambda}$ are known over the interval $d\lambda$, photocurrent I_P is then

$$I_P = R(\lambda)\ \Phi_{E\lambda}\ d\lambda$$

where I_P is in amperes.

If R was given a value in amperes per lumen (A/lm), the I_P would be

$$I_P = R\Phi_V$$

where I_P is in amperes and Φ_V is the total incident luminous flux.

If the radiant flux is a band of wavelengths,

$$\Phi_E = \int_{\leq 1}^{\lambda_2} \Phi_{E\lambda}\ d\lambda$$

where Φ_E is expressed in watts (W). In this instance, the responsivity is in terms of amperes/watt, so

$$I_P = R\Phi_E$$

Measuring Quantum Efficiency

Our next interest lies in the quantum efficiency of a photodetector. A quantum efficiency (Q.E.) of unity implies that one photoelectron is emitted or one electron-hole pair is generated for every incident quantum. With detectors, the Q.E. is usually defined at some particular wavelength; therefore Q.E.(λ) is the ratio of the number of photoelectrons per second to the number of incident quanta at particular wavelength per second. Thus the number of photoelectrons per second is

$$I_P/e = R(\lambda)\ \Phi_{E\lambda}\ d\lambda/e$$

where e is the charge of an electron $(1.6021917 \times 10^{-19}$ coulomb). Therefore, the Q.E. is

$$Q.E.(\lambda) = R(\lambda)\ hc/e\lambda$$

and since $hc/e = 1.23985 \times 10^{-6}$ watts per milliampere,

$$Q.E.(\lambda) = 1.23985 \times 10^{-6}\ R(\lambda)/\lambda$$

where λ is in microns.

The terms Φ_E and Φ_V are general terms and may be qualified to represent values at specific wavelengths, as luminous flux $\Phi_{V\lambda}$ and radiant flux $\Phi_{E\lambda}$. Their ratio at a given wavelength λ is the *spectral luminous efficacy*, $K(\lambda)$.

231

Appendix A
Useful Graphs
and Tables

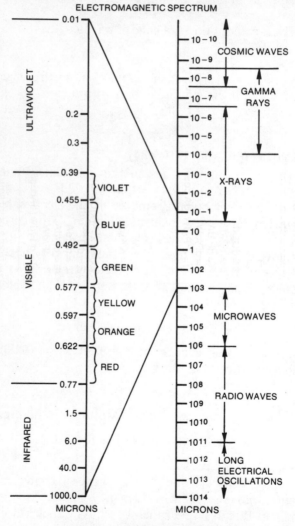

Electromagnetic Spectrum

Radiometric Parameters

PARAMETER	SYMBOL	DEFINITION	UNIT	ABBREVIATION
RADIOMETRIC PARAMETERS				
Radiant energy	Q_E	—	Joule (erg)	J
Radiant flux	P	$P=dQ_E/dt$	Erg/Sec	erg/sec
Radiant emittance	W	$W=dP/dA$	Watts/cm²	W/cm²
Irradiance	H	$H=dP/dA$	Watts/cm²	W/cm²
Radiant intensity	J	$J=dP/dW$	Watt/Steracian	W/sr
Radiance	N	$N=d^2P/dW\,(dA\cos\theta)$	Watt/sr and cm²	W/sr-cm²
PHOTOMETRIC PARAMETERS				
Luminous efficacy	K	$K=F/W$	Lumen/watt	lm/W
Luminous efficiency	V	$V=K/K_{MAX}$		
Luminous energy	Q_V	$Q_V=\int k^{F60}(\lambda)Q_{E\lambda}d\lambda$	Lumen-hour	lm-h
Luminous flux	F	$F=dQ^{380}_V/dt$	Lumen	lm
Luminous emittance	L	$L=dF/dA$	Lumen/ft²	lm/ft²
Illuminance	E	$E=dF/dA$	Footcandle	fc
Luminous intensity	I	$I=dF/dW$	Candela	cd
Luminance	B	$B=d^2F/dw\,(dA\cos\theta)$	Candela/area	cd/in²

w = is a solid angle through which flux from a point source is radiated
θ = is the angle between line of sight and normal to surface considered
λ = wavelength
W and L = emitted from
H and E = incident on

Comparison of Different Photosensitive Devices

PARAMETER	PHOTOTRANSISTOR	PHOTODIODE	PHOTO-SCR	PHOTOCELLS	
				Si	CdSi/CdSe
P_D	50–400 mW	50 mW	2.0W	400 mW	50 mW to 25W
I	1–50 mA	50–200 µA	1.4A	1.0A	10 mA to 1.0A
f	200 kHz	200 kHz (1)	1 kHz	50 kHz	1 kHz
t_r/t_f	2–100 µsec	2 µsec	2 µsec	100 µSec	100 msec
Spectral response	V to IR	V to IR	V to IR	V to IR	V to IR
Colour sensitivity		increases towards red; decreases towards blue			
V_{MAX}	50V	100V	200V	(**)	100V
$T_{a(MAX)}$	125°C	125°C	100°C	150°C	75°C
Directional I flow	uni	uni	uni	uni	bi
Hysteresis	no	no	no	no	yes (3)
Stability	good	excellent	good	excellent	poor to good
Light levels	0.001–20 mW/cm²	0.001–200 mW/cm²	2–200 mW/cm²	0.001 mW to 1W/cm²	(46)

Notes:

1—PIN photodiodes f=10 mHz 2— depending on type 3— exposure to bright levels alters sensitivity 4— depending on type

Abbreviations:

P_D= power dissipation I= current f= frequency response t_r= rise time t_f= fall time V_{MAX}= maximum applied voltage $T_{a(MAX)}$= maximum operating temperature uni= unidirectional bi= bidirectional

Comparison of Different Emitters

	LED	LCD (dynamic)	LCD (field effect)	GAS DISCHARGE	FLUORESCENT CRT	SEGMENT	INCANDESCENT
Model	A	P	P	A	A	A	A
Voltage	1.5V	15V	5V	200V	2.5 kV	15V	6.3V
Current	10 mA	0.003 mA	0.3 µA	0.2 mA	0.035 mA	0.1 mA	250 mA
Speed	fast	Medium	Medium	Fast	Fast	Fast	Slow
Wattage	15 mW	0.045 mW	0.0015 mW	40 mW			

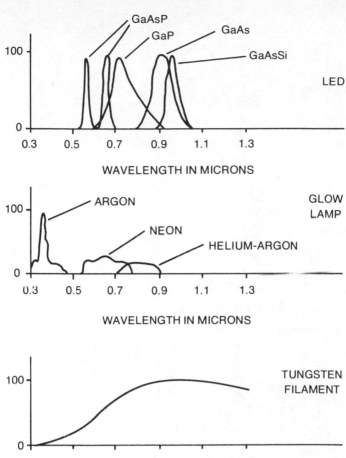

LED

WAVELENGTH IN MICRONS

GLOW LAMP

WAVELENGTH IN MICRONS

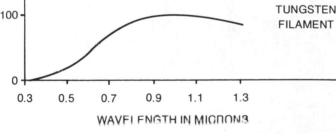

TUNGSTEN FILAMENT

WAVELENGTH IN MICRONS

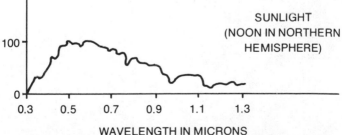

SUNLIGHT (NOON IN NORTHERN HEMISPHERE)

WAVELENGTH IN MICRONS

SPECTRAL DISTRIBUTION OF COMMON SOURCES

Relative Spectral Distribution of Common Sources (continued on page 236)

235

2856°K TUNGSTEN LAMP

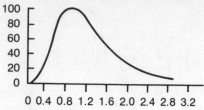

150W XENON ARC (SHORT)

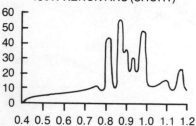

FLUORESCENT LAMP (DAYLIGHT)

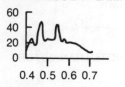

CARBON ARC

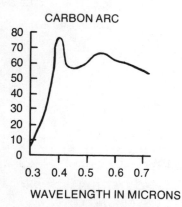

WAVELENGTH IN MICRONS

Relative Spectral Distribution of Common Sources (Continued)

236

RELATIVE RESPONSE OF DETECTORS

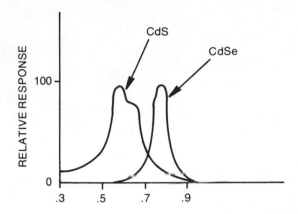

WAVELENGTH IN MICRONS

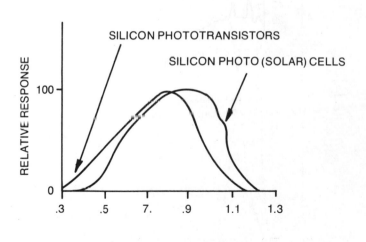

WAVELENGTH IN MICRONS

Relative Response of Detectors

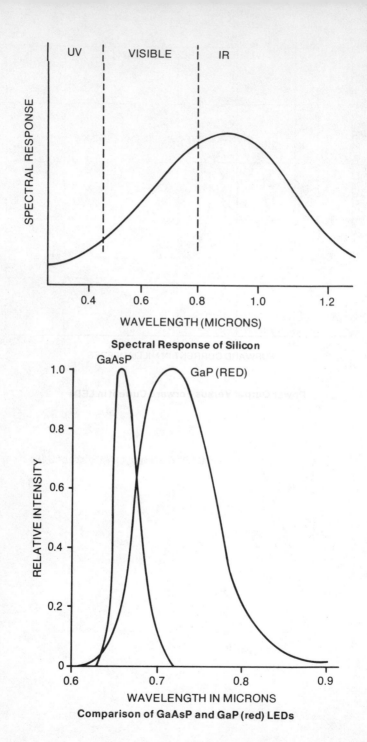

Spectral Response of Silicon

Comparison of GaAsP and GaP (red) LEDs

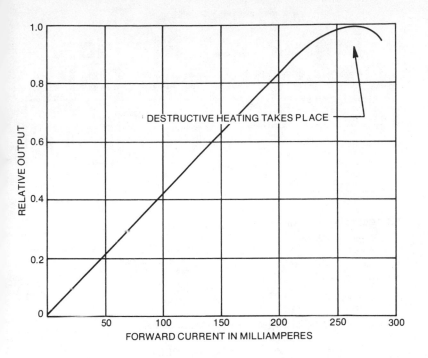

Power Output Versus Forward Current in LEDs

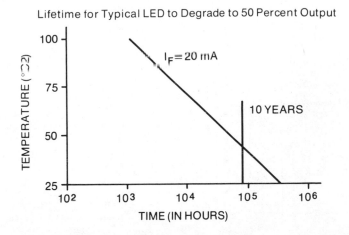

Lifetime for Typical LED to Degrade to 50 Percent Output

Lifetime for Typical LED to Degrade to 50 Percent Output

239

Appendix B
Important Physical Constants and Units

QUANTITY	SYMBOL	VALUE	UNIT
Boltzmann's constant	k	1.380622×10^{-23}	JK^{-1}
electron charge	e	$1.6021917 \times 10^{-16}$	C
energy of 1 electron volt	eV	$1.6021917 \times 10^{-16}$	J
Planck's constant	h	6.626196×10^{-34}	Js
velocity of light	c	2.9979250×10^{8}	m/s

UNITS	SYMBOL	DEFINITION
ampere	A	unit of electric current
angstrom	A°	$1 A° = 10^{-10} m$
barn	b	$1 b = 10^{-28} m^2$
bit	b	the unit of information ($\log_2 N$), where N is the maximum number of possible states for a storage device.
candela	cd	unit of luminous intensity
candela per m^2	cd/m^2	unit of luminance (often called "nit")
candle	cd	same as candela
coulomb	C	unit of electronic charge
cycle per second	Hz	unit of frequency
degree	°	unit of angle ($1° = 0.017453$ rad)
dyne	dyn	unit of force
electron volt	eV	energy of an electron possessed by acceleration through a potential difference of one volt
erg	erg	unit of energy
farad	F	unit of capacitance
footcandle	fc	lumen/ft^2 or (lumen/m^2 called "lux")
footlambert	fL	unit of luminance ($1 fL = (1/\pi)$ cd/ft^2), but cd/m^2 is preferred
gauss	G	unit of magnetic flux density
henry	H	unit of inductance
hertz	Hz	unit of frequency
joule	J	unit of energy
kelvin	K	unit of temperature
kilogram	kg	unit of mass
lambert	L	unit of luminance (cd/m^2 is preferred)
lumen	lm	unit of luminous flux
lumen per ft^2	lm/ft^2	unit of illuminance
lumen per m^2	lm/m^2	unit of luminous exitance
lumen per watt	lm/W	unit of luminous efficacy
lumen second	lm-s	unit of quantity of light (talbot)
lux	lx	unit of illuminance ($1 lx = 1 lm/m^2$)
meter	m	unit of length
micron	μ	$10^{-6} m$
mil	mil	0.001 inch
mole	mol	unit of substance
newton	N	unit of force
ohm	Ω	unit of resistance
pascal	Pa	$Pa = N/m^2$
radian	rad	unit of plane angle (1 rad $= 57.2958$ deg.)
second	s or sec	unit of time
siemens	S	unit of conductance
sterdian	sr	unit of solid angle
stokes	St	unit of viscosity
tesla	T	unit of magnetic induction
volt	V	unit of voltage
watt	W	unit of power
weber	Wb	unit of magnetic flux

Appendix C
Optoelectronic Device Characteristics

The following tables give general characteristics for different opto-electronic devices. Abbreviations for manufacturers are as follows:

Fairchild—F
Litronix—LI
General Electric—GE
Hewlett Packard—HP
Monsanto—M
Opcoa—OP
Clairex—CL

Light-Emitting Diode Characteristics

TYPE	MFG.	PEAK RESPONSE (angstroms)	V_F	$I_F(mA)$	V_R
FLD100	F	9000	1.25	800	2
FLV100	F	6500	1.8	50	3
FLV106	F	6500	1.6	40	3
SSL3	GE	5390	1.4	100	2
SSL4	GE	9000	1.25	800	2
SSL5A	GE	9400	1.35	500	2
SSL12	GE	6500	1.6	40	3
SSL15	GE	6600	1.65	50	3
SSL22/L	GE	6500	1.8	50	3
SSL55B	GE	9000	1.25	800	2
5082-4106	HP	9000	1.25	800	2
5082-4107	HP	9000	1.2	150	3
5082-4400	HP	6500	1.8	50	3
LIT2	LI	6500	1.8	50	3
LIT5	LI	6100	2.0	70	3
LIT7	LI	6600	1.65	50	3
LIT60	LI	9000	1.2	80	3
LIT209	LI	6500	1.6	40	3
IRL40	LI	9000	1.25	800	2
ME60	M	9000	1.2	80	2
MV1	M	6100	2.0	70	3
MV2	M	5390	1.4	100	2
MV3	M	6500	1.8	50	3
MV10	M	6600	1.65	50	3
MV5074	M	6500	1.6	40	3
OSL-1	OP	6100	2.0	70	3
OSL-2	OP	6500	1.8	50	3
ME1	M	9000	1.3	100	3
ME4	M	9000	1.25	800	2
ME6	M	9300	1.25	100	2

Phototransistor Characteristics

TYPE	MFG.	BV$_{CEO}$(V)	P$_D$(mW)	Iceo (mA)	PEAK RESPONSE (angstroms)
CLR2050	CL	50	250	0.025	8000
CLT2020	CL	30	200	0.01	8200
CLT3160	CL	50	50	0.025	8000
CLT3170	CL	50	50	0.025	8000
FPF110/A	F	30	200	0.02	8000
FPF130/A	F	20	200	0.01	8000
FPM100	F	50	50	0.025	8000
FPT100/A	F	30	200	0.02	8000
FPT120	F	20	200	0.01	8000
FPT120A	F	50	50	0.025	8000
MT1	M	30	400	5.0	8000
MT2	M	30	200	0.01	8200
L14A	GE	30	175	0.01	8250
L14B1	GE	40	200	0.1	8500
L14B3	GE	40	200	0.1	8500
L14B4	GE	40	100	0.1	8000
L14D1	GE	40	250	0.1	8500
L14D3	GE	40	250	0.1	8500

Readouts/Displays Characteristics

TYPE	MFG.	CHARACTER HEIGHT (inches)	I/SEGMENT (mA)	FEATURES
FND10/a	F	0.12	10	CC, SS
FND21	F	0.35	20/diode	alphanumeric
SSL140	GE	0.12	10	CC, SS
SSL190	GE	0.27	30	CA, SS
5082-7000	HP	0.27	30	CA, SS
5082-7018	HP	0.27	30	PI
5082-7100	HP	0.35	20/diode	alphanumeric
SLA-1	OP	0.27	30	CA, SS
SLA-2	OP	0.27	30	PI
DL10	LI	0.27	30	CA, SS
DL30	LI	0.12	10	CC, SS
DL101	LI	0.27	30	PI
MAN1	M	0.27	30	CA, SS
MAN1A	M	0.27	30	CA, SS
MAN2	M	0.35	20/diode	alphanumeric
MAN3	M	0.12	10	CC, SS
MAN1001	M	0.27	30	PI
MAN1001A	M	0.27	30	PI

CC—Common cathode
CA—Common anode
SS—Seven-segment
PI—Polarity indicator

Optically Coupled Isolator Characteristics

TYPE	MFG.	EMITTER VOLTAGE	EMITTER CURRENT (mA)	CURRENT TRANSFER RATIO	ISOLATION VOLTAGE
IL-1	LI	1.25	60	50	1500
IL-2	LI	1.2	10	200	1500
IL-6	LI	1.25	60	14	1500
MCA2-30	M	100	2	—	3000
MCD-1	M	1.25	60	50	1500
MCT-26	M	1.25	60	14	1500
5082-4301	HP	1.2	35	—	5000
FCD810	F	1.25	60	50	1500
FCD820	F	1.2	10	200	1500

Photoconductive Sensor Characteristics

TYPE	MFG.	PEAK RESPONSE (angstoms)	DARK RESISTANCE (megohms)	V_P(MAX)	P_D(mW)
CL2P	CL	5500	160	250	100
CL3	CL	7200	3000	250	100
CL4	CL	7200	3000	250	100

243

Appendix D
Glossary

acceptor—an atom inserted into a semiconductor to accept an electron from the semiconductor.

AND gate—a logic circuit which requires that all inputs be in the "on" state to generate the "on" output state.

angular alignment—a measure of the deviation of the optical axis from the mechanical axis.

area source—a source with a diameter greater than 10 percent of the distance between it and a detector.

avalanche transistor—a transistor which when operated at a high reverse-bias voltage will supply a chain generation of electron-hole pairs.

baffle—a single shielding device designed to reduce the effect of ambient light on an optical emitter/detector unit.

bandgap energy—the difference in energy between the conduction band and the valence band.

blackbody—a 100-percent efficient radiator and absorber of radiant energy.

bias—voltage applied to a solid-state device.

breakdown voltage—the reverse-bias voltage applied to a PN junction for which large currents are drawn for relatively small increases in voltage.

coherent radiation—radiation whose waves are in phase in respect to time and space.

conduction band—a partially filled energy band of a material in which electrons can move freely, thus allowing the material to carry an electric current.

conductivity—a measure of a material's ability to carry an electric current.

conversion efficiency—the ratio of maximum available radiant flux output to total input power.

continuous wave (CW)—uninterrupted forward-current operation.

critical angle—the maximum angle of incidence for which light will be transmitted from one medium to another. Light approaching the interface at angles greater than the critical angle will be reflected back into the first medium.

dark current—the current that flows in a photodetector when there is no incident radiation on the detector.

DC transfer ratio—the ratio of the DC output current to the DC input current.

Darlington amplifier—a composite configuration of transistors that provides a high input impedance and a high degree of amplification.

Darlington phototransistor—a phototransistor whose collector and emitter are connected to a second transistor, creating very high sensitivity.

delay time—the time interval from the point at which the leading edge of the input pulse has reached 10 percent of its maximum amplitude to the point at which the leading edge of the output pulse has reached 10 percent of its maximum amplitude.

diode—a semiconductor device which passes current in only one direction.

direct material—a semiconductor material in which electrons drop from the conduction band directly to the valence band to recombine with holes. This recombination process conserves energy and momentum.

discrete—refers to an individual circuit component, complete in itself.

donor—an atom inserted into a semiconductor to donate an electron to the semiconductor.

doping—the process of inserting impurity atoms (donors or acceptors) into an intrinsic semiconductor to alter the electrical properties of the host material.

duty cycle—a measure of the effect of a pulsed input to a device, expressed as a percentage of on time as compared to total time.

duty factor—same as "duty cycle" except expressed as a decimal rather than a percentage.

dv/dt—the rate of change of voltage with respect to time.

electroluminescence—in a semiconductor, the direct conversion of electrical energy into light.

epitaxial—new layers of atoms deposited on a host material in such a manner that the new (epitaxial) layer perpetuates the crystalline structure of the host substrate.

fall time—the time duration during which the trailing edge of a pulse is decreasing from 90 percent to 10 percent of its maximum amplitude.

f number—a number that describes a lens; the ratio of focal length to lens diameter.

flip-flop—a logic circuit with two inputs and two corresponding stable states.

flux—power passing through a surface (energy per unit time).

forbidden gap—in the band theory of solids, the range of energies between the conduction and the valence bands; electrons cannot exist at energies in this range.

hole—in a semiconductor the term is used to describe the absence of an electron.

incandescence—the generation of light caused by passing an electric current through a filament.

indirect material—semiconductor material in which electrons do not drop directly from the conduction to the valence band, but drop in steps due to the trapping levels in the forbidden gap.

infrared radiation—radiation in the wavelength range of 0.78 microns to approximately 100.0 microns.

intrinsic characteristics—characteristics of a material that are due to the material itself and not dependent on impurities.

intrinsic material—semiconductor material that has an equal number of electrons and holes.

IRED—infrared light-emitting diode.

LASCR—light-activated, silicon-controlled rectifier.

LASCS—light-activated, silicon-controlled switch.

LASER—a device that produces high-energy coherent light. In the case of a semiconductor, a mechanically designed junction that will optically pump (amplify) short pulses.

lattice—a three-dimensional pattern of atoms that is repeated throughout a single crystal.

LED—light-emitting diode.

light—visually evaluated radiant energy with wavelengths from 0.38 to 0.78 microns.

light-emitting diode—a diode that emits visible radiant energy.

light-emitting diode, infrared—a diode that emits infrared radiant energy from 0.78 to 100 microns in wavelength.

luminescence—emission of light due to any cause other than high temperatures.

magnification ratio—in reference to lens, the image size divided by source size.

micron—a unit of distance equal to one-millionth of a meter.

modulation—a varying of the characteristics of a wave by controlling it with another wave.

monochromatic—having one color, and thus one frequency or wavelength.

N-type material—semiconductor material having electrons as the majority charge carriers.

noncoherent radiation—radiation whose waves are out of phase with respect to time and space.

optical axis—a line about which the radiant energy pattern is centered, usually perpendicular to the active area.

optically coupled isolator—a device consisting of an emitter and a detector integrated into a single entity, which is used to transfer a signal from the input to the output via radiant energy.

optoelectronics—any circuit involving solid-state emitters or detectors.

OR gate—a logic circuit that requires that at least one input be in the "on" state to drive the output into the "on" state.

P-type material—semiconductor material having holes as the majority charge carriers.

peak spectral emission—that wavelength at which a material radiates its highest intensity.

phonon—quantum of thermal energy.

phosphor—any material that emits radiant energy when excited by radiant energy, though electron bombardment is commonly used.

photoconductor—light-sensitive resistor.

photodetector—any device that senses incident radiation.

photodiode—a solid-state device that requires incident light on the PN junction for the device to conduct.

photon—quantum of light.

phototransistor—solid-state device similiar to a conventional transistor except light incident of the PN junction controls the response of this device, which also offers built-in gain.

PN junction—the interface between P-type and N-type materials.

point source—radiation source whose maximum dimension is less than 10 percent of the distance between emitter and detector.

potential gradient—voltage gradient due to the diffusion of holes and electrons across the space charge region.

relative detector response—a plot showing how the response varies with wavelength.

resistivity—a measure of a material's resistance to the flow of electric current.

SCR—silicon controlled rectifier.

SCS—silicon controlled switch.

space charge region—the region around a PN junction in which holes and electrons recombine, leaving no mobile charge carriers and a net charge difference other than zero.

spectral distribution of energy—a plot showing the variation of spectral emission with reference to wavelength.

steradian—solid angle subtending an area on the surface of a sphere equal to the square of the radius.

thermal equilibrium—condition in which a system and its surroundings are at the same temperature.

threshold voltage—voltage at which a PN junction begins to pass an electric current.

transition region—region around a PN junction in which the majority carriers of each side diffuse across the junction to recombine.

transmittance—the ratio of the radiant power emitted by a body to the total radiant power received by the body.

valence band—in a semiconductor, the band of energies just below the conduction band, separated from it by the forbidden gap.

Index